ST(P) MATHEMATICS

Teacher's Notes and Answers

L. Bostock, B.Sc.

formerly Senior Mathematics Lecturer, Southgate Technical College

S. Chandler, B.Sc.

formerly of the Godolphin and Latymer School

A. Shepherd, B.Sc.

Head of Mathematics, Redland High School for Girls

E. Smith, M.Sc.

Head of Mathematics, Tredegar Comprehensive School

Stanley Thornes (Publishers) Ltd

First published 1987 by
Stanley Thornes (Publishers) Ltd,
Old Station Drive,
Leckhampton,
CHELTENHAM GL53 0DN

Reprinted 1987

British Library Cataloguing in Publication Data
ST(P) mathematics 4B.
 Teacher's notes and answer book
 1. Mathematics — 1961 –
 I. Bostock, L.
 510   QA39.2

ISBN 0–85950–253–8

Typeset by KEYTEC, Bridport, Dorset
Printed and bound in Great Britain by Ebenezer Baylis & Son, Worcester

ST(P) MATHEMATICS 4B
Teacher's Notes and Answers

ST(P) MATHEMATICS will be completed as follows:

Published 1984
- ST(P) 1
- ST(P) 1   Teacher's Notes and Answers
- ST(P) 2

Published 1985
- ST(P) 2   Teacher's Notes and Answers
- ST(P) 3A
- ST(P) 3B
- ST(P) 3A   Teacher's Notes and Answers
- ST(P) 3B   Teacher's Notes and Answers

Published 1986
- ST(P) 4A
- ST(P) 4B
- ST(P) 4A   Teacher's Notes and Answers
- ST(P) 4B   Teacher's Notes and Answers

Published 1987
- ST(P) 5A   (with answers)
- ST(P) 5B   (with answers)

In preparation
- ST(P) 5C   (with answers)
- ST(P)   Resource Book

INTRODUCTION

This book is intended for pupils aiming at the intermediate papers in GCSE Mathematics, and covers most of the work common to all syllabuses.

Although there is some new work in this book, much of the content uses basic processes introduced in earlier books but now applied to a wide variety of everyday situations.

ST(P) 5B completes the course for the written papers at intermediate level.

Candidates who are certain to be taking the foundation level papers can proceed directly to 5C where all the work necessary for that level is contained.

Many of the questions contain ideas which can be broadened into extended pieces of work or can form the basis of a project. The detailed notes which follow have some specific suggestions.

Questions that are double underlined, e.g. <u><u>2</u></u>, are harder than the others and require problem solving ability. They should be used with caution although they are good for class discussion.

Questions that are single underlined, e.g. <u>2</u>, are extra, but not harder, questions for further practice or revision.

We have continued to use multiple choice questions where appropriate because we feel that they offer opportunities for discussion. Also, because they should be worked through quickly, without time for calculations, they encourage estimation and consideration of whether or not an answer is reasonable.

NOTES AND ANSWERS

CHAPTER 1   Change of Units

EXERCISE 1a   Gives practice in changing units in the metric system. It helps if units are related to familiar objects, e.g. a 5 ml medicine spoon, 1 kg bag of sugar.

1.	5300 g	**11.**	0.856 litres	**21.**	0.372 km
2.	860 mm^2	**12.**	2.5 kg	**22.**	56 mm^2
3.	7300 mm	**13.**	0.8976 hectares	**23.**	8 270 000 cm^3
4.	1500 ml	**14.**	0.028 m^3	**24.**	39 litres
5.	3000 mm^3	**15.**	2.56 m	**25.**	0.025 t
6.	260 kg	**16.**	2.93 litres	**26.**	10.5 cm^2
7.	8000 m^2	**17.**	0.187 t	**27.**	2720 ml
8.	2500 cm	**18.**	0.825 m^3	**28.**	960 m
9.	500 ml	**19.**	5.93 cm^2	**29.**	3250 kg
10.	700 cm^3	**20.**	8.26 m	**30.**	0.2998 m^3

31.	628 g	**35.**	37 cm^3	**39.**	200 000 mm^3
32.	0.5 hectare	**36.**	0.4 litres	**40.**	800 cm^2
33.	0.08 cm^3	**37.**	82 t		
34.	9620 mm	**38.**	0.37 km		

41.	a) 8000 cm^3	b) 8000 ml	c) 0.008 m^3
42.	a) 35 000 cm	b) 0.35 km	c) 350 000 mm
43.	a) 3.5 m^2	b) 3 500 000 mm^2	
44.	a) 600 cm^3	b) 600 ml	c) 0.0006 m^3
45.	a) 85 000 mm	b) 85 m	c) 0.085 km
46.	a) 470 cm^2	b) 47 000 mm^2	
47.	a) 5 500 000 mm^3	b) 0.0055 m^3	
48.	a) 3.5×10^8 mm^3	b) 3.5×10^{-1} m^3	c) 3.5×10^2 litres
49.	a) 1.6×10^8 mm^2	b) 1.6×10^{-2} hectares	c) 1.6×10^{-4} km^2
50.	a) 7.3×10^{12} cm^2	b) 7.3×10^2 km^2	c) 7.3×10^4 hectares

EXERCISE 1b   Gives practice in changing imperial units. This may be unfamiliar ground for many pupils and everyday examples will be helpful, e.g. a 1 pint milk bottle, a 1 lb bag of apples from a greengrocer. A general discussion and investigation on the mixture of units in current use is sensible at this stage— e.g. prepacked goods are nearly all sold in kilograms and grams but loose fruit and vegetables are sold by the pound and ounce.

1.	24 in	**5.**	24 stones	**9.**	3 ft
2.	4 pints	**6.**	12 oz	**10.**	2 lb
3.	21 lb	**7.**	30 in	**11.**	2 gallons
4.	6 ft	**8.**	24 oz	**12.**	4 yd

13. 1 ft 6 in   **14.** 1 lb 4 oz   **15.** 1 gallon 4 pints   **16.** 4 stones

17. a) 288 in   b) 8 yd
18. a) $\frac{1}{4}$ b) $\frac{9}{16}$
19. a) 36 in   b) 18 in   c) $4\frac{1}{2}$ in
20. a) 8 oz   b) 12 oz   c) 2 oz
21. a) $\frac{1}{2}$ b) $\frac{3}{4}$
22. a) 16 pints   b) 14 pints
23. a) 16 stones   b) 2 cwt
24. a) $\frac{2}{3}$ b) $\frac{7}{9}$
25. a) 432 sq in   b) $\frac{1}{3}$ sq yd

EXERCISE 1c   **1.** 15 minutes   **5.** 604 800 seconds   **9.** 8760 hours
2. 50 minutes   **6.** 22 hours   **10.** 43 200 minutes
3. $1\frac{1}{2}$ hours   **7.** 8 weeks
4. $1\frac{1}{2}$ days   **8.** 1440 minutes

11. a) 27 minutes   b) 28 minutes   c) 1 hour 22 minutes
12. a) 24 minutes   b) 14 minutes
13. a) 4 trains   b) 5 hours   c) 34 minutes

EXERCISE 1d This exercise illustrates the type of everyday situation where conversion between metric and imperial units may arise. These questions have, deliberately, no instructions on how precisely to give the answers and we have left it for the users to decide for themselves. It is very necessary, however, to know what is, and what is not, a reasonable answer. This could be introduced, for example, with a motorist driving on the continent and seeing a speed limit of 35 km/hr and needing to convert that into m.p.h. Using 5 miles ≃ 8 km and a calculator gives 21.875 m.p.h., but all that the driver needs to know is the speed limit to within 1 or 2 m.p.h. So 22 m.p.h, or 20 m.p.h, are perfectly reasonable answers whereas 21.875 m.p.h. is not because no driver can measure his speed to 3 s.f. Besides, 5 miles is not *exactly* 8 km so 21.875 is not even accurate.

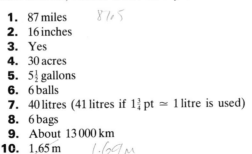

1. 87 miles   *87.5*
2. 16 inches
3. Yes
4. 30 acres
5. $5\frac{1}{2}$ gallons
6. 6 balls
7. 40 litres (41 litres if $1\frac{3}{4}$ pt ≃ 1 litre is used)
8. 6 bags
9. About 13 000 km
10. 1.65 m   *1.69 M*

EXERCISE 1e Many of these problems require decisions on how many figures to give for a reasonable answer.

  1. a) 0.5 km/min   b) 30 000 m/h
  2. a) 0.1 km/s   b) 6000 m/min   c) 6 km/min
  3. a) 80 m.p.h. (81 m.p.h.)
  4. 31 ft/sec
  5. 110 km/h (112 km/h)
  6. 36.1 m/s (3 s.f.)
  7. 72 km/h
  8. 44 ft/sec
  9. 7.5 litres/sec
10. 28 m.p.g
11. 500 miles
12. 25 m²
13. 24 sq yd
14. 25 ml/shampoo
15. a) 300   b) 12
16. 12 gallons (11.25 gallons)
17. 15 gallons
18. 20 miles/litre
19. 11 km/litre (10.7 km/litre to 3 s.f.)
20. 27 lb/sq in (27.5)

EXERCISE 1f Gives practice in using conversion graphs. Again discuss the accuracy of answers; in the worked example, for instance, is 37 °C exactly 98.5 °F? Also, with particular emphasis on the approximate nature of conversion graphs, discuss how the size of the graph can affect the accuracy of readings from it.

  1. a) 320 km   b) 375 miles   c) 270 miles (approx)
  2. a) 11 km/litre
     b) 51 m.p.g.; 42 m.p.g. = 15 km/litre, 26 m.p.g. = 9 km/litre
  3. a) 7 oz   b) 143 g   c) 4 oz packet of sweets
  4. a) 2.8 litre   b) 7 pints   c) 1.3 pints   d) 9 litres
  5. 230 oz flour, 115 g castor sugar, 85 g butter, 58 g sultanas, 2 eggs
  6. a) 1 litres ≃ 1.75 pints   b) 7000 pints
  7. 58 °F ≃ 14 °C, 36 °F ≃ 2 °C   a) 22 °F b) 12 °C
  8. a) 58 cm   b) 6 in   c) 38 cm

EXERCISE 1g **1.** a) i) $76   ii) $38   b) i) £69   ii) £33
           2. a) £16   b) 1100 pta   c) £12.50   d) 3300 pta
           3. a) 6 f   b) £2   c) £2.75
              d) Yes: at 10 p each he would get £2.50 if he sold all the sweets and
                £2.50 ≃ 27 f.
           4. 20 p
           5. 47.5 f

EXERCISE 1h   When some conversion graphs have been drawn, it is sensible to ask pupils to criticise a badly drawn conversion graph.

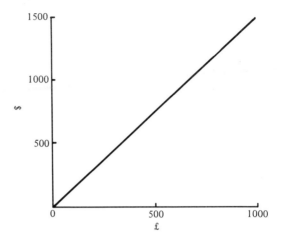

For instance you could show them a graph like this, on plain unlined paper, with a thick line graph and ask them whether it is easy to read or if it is any use to someone on holiday or could it be used to find the equivalent of $100 in £, etc.

(Graphs in questions 1–5 drawn to $\frac{1}{4}$ scale)

1. a) i) 120 Ff   ii) 1200 Ff   **2.** a) i) $2.60   ii) $13

b)   b)

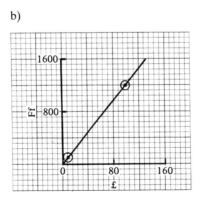   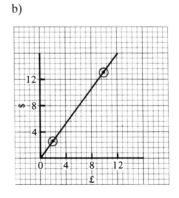

c) i) 660 Ff   ii) £83   c) i) $3.25   ii) £3.80

3. a) i) 10 DM = 35 f
   ii) 100 DM = 350 f

b)

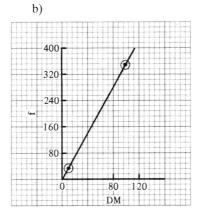

c) i) 385 f
   ii) 80 DM

5. a) i) 10 in ≡ 25 cm
   ii) 100 in ≡ 250 cm

b)

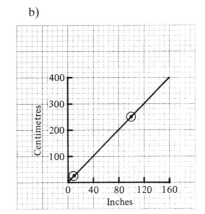

c) i) 140 inches
   ii) 100 cm

4. a) i) 215 p   ii) 430 p

b)

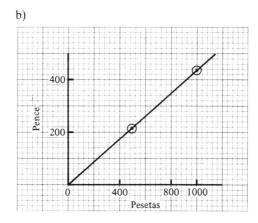

c) i) 580 pta   ii) £3.90

EXERCISE 1i **1.** a) 190 cm   b) 0.25 kg
2. a) 48 inches   b) 4 lb
3. 53 minutes
4. 96 km
5. 64 km/hour
6. 111 gallons

EXERCISE 1j   **1.** a) 0.5 litres   b) 500 mm²   **4.** 5.5 lb
   2. a) 24 pints   b) 6 yards   **5.** a) 12   b) 36
   3. 27 minutes   **6.** Yes, the cloth is 100 inches long.

EXERCISE 1k   **1. B**   **2. D**   **3. C**   **4. D**   **5. A**

CHAPTER 2   Reading Tables

This chapter contains various samples of tabulated information but these are only small extracts from larger documents. Pupils should be able to see and use complete holiday brochures, railway timetables, conversion tables, etc. These can be used to advantage for projects, e.g. planning outings, holidays, journeys, etc.

EXERCISE 2a   **1.** a) 4   b) i) 180°C   ii) 350°F   c) gas mark 5
   2. shirt, size 42; shoes, size 43; 16
   3. a) 14   b) too big   c) 87 cm
   4. a) (i) 33°C   (ii) 90°F   b) 22°C   c) 109°F

EXERCISE 2b   **1.** a) 174 DM   b) £2.32   **4.** a) £4.65   b) 30 638 lira
   2. a) 525 drachmas   b) £5.11   **5.** a) 398 schillings   b) £4.30
   3. a) US$ 137   b) £5.21

   6. £8.21   **9.** £0.47   **12.** £10.74
   7. £9.88   **10.** £3.17   **13.** £11.53
   8. £95.33   **11.** £25.45   **14.** £0.84

   15. 6.33 Ff   **18.** 2.88 Ff   **21.** 452.1 DM
   16. £0.30   **19.** 0.35 DM   **22.** 6.25 DM
   17. £0.67   **20.** 228 Ff   **23.** US$ 19.09

EXERCISE 2c   **1.** 03.20   **4.** 22.40   **7.** 21.13
   2. 11.52   **5.** 12.00   **8.** 09.13
   3. 13.00   **6.** 01.00   **9.** 23.59

   10. 2.30 p.m.   **13.** 8.20 p.m.   **16.** 2.06 a.m.
   11. 9.15 a.m.   **14.** 0.01 a.m.   **17.** 10.45 a.m.
   12. 11.20 a.m.   **15.** 4.25 p.m.   **18.** 11.18 p.m.

   19. 19 hours 55 minutes
   20. 8 hours 29 minutes
   21. 4 hours 16 minutes
   22. 5 hours 47 minutes
   23. a) 11.45, morning   b) 15.30, afternoon,   c) 01.15, morning
   24. a) 15.08   b) 19.15; 07.00

EXERCISE 2d   In this chapter, times from a 24-hour clock are mainly given in the form 12.00 rather than 1200. The majority of, but not all, timetables and brochures use this form so pupils should be familiar with it, as well as the 1200 form used in earlier books.

1. a) 1st bus 2 h 22 min, 2nd bus 2 h 17 min
  b) 1st bus 19 min, 2nd bus 14 min
2. a) Red Farm Hill and Astleton
  b) Astleton and Morgans Hollow
3. a) 4 hours 49 minutes
  b) 6 hours 33 minutes
4. a) 3
  b) 20.31 (She need not have left Taunton until 19.27)
  c) 47 minutes
5. a) 35 minutes   b) 55 minutes
6. a) 35 minutes   b) Murder, Mystery and Suspense on ITV.
           1 hour 45 minutes
7. 5 minutes
8. a) The Collectors or Murder, Mystery and Suspense
  b) 35 minutes
9. The Collectors and News, Sport and Weather
10. 12-hour clock, the programmes are in the evening but the times do not exceed 12; adding p.m.

11. a) 1   b) 7
12. a) 3   b) 4   c) The 17.14 from King's Cross
13. a) 2 minutes   b) 24 minutes
  c) 15 minutes   d) 8 minutes
14. a) 17.34
  b) Yes, he can get off at Finsbury Park and catch the 17.19 from there to Oakleigh Park, he arrives 7 minutes later.
15. a) 12 minutes, 17.39
  b) 38 minutes

EXERCISE 2e   Much interesting work and discussion can arise from this exercise. Pupils can produce their own brochures and plan economical holidays etc.

1. a) £83 each   b) £72 each
  c) No, they are not taking a two-week holiday so they do not qualify for a free week.
2. a) 4 Jan to 7 Jan   b) £153 for 3 weeks from 8 Jan to 23 Jan

3. a) i) £30   ii) £21
  b) i) £134   ii) £153   iii) £128
4. a) £854   b) £49   c) i) £245   ii) £426
5. a) i) £146   ii) £200   b) 1 week A_2 or A_4
  c) Group D Nationwide costs are £250 against £240 for 3 weeks in Florida, £10

6. a) £325   b) £404

7. £661.50; 017 X

8. £336

9. a) £816   b) £260   c) £1712

10. a) 21, 28 June, 5, 12, 19 July

      b) £573.80 at the Royal leaving 21 or 28 June

      c) No, the cheapest holiday at Montana costs £700.80   d) £589.80

11. a) £894.60   b) £924.75

12. Majestic, 19 May

13. a) £861   b) £906

EXERCISE 2f   The temperature chart in questions 1 to 3 is deliberately left as vague as it was in the original brochure. Although the questions ask only for temperature *differences*, it is worth asking pupils if they can state the actual temperature at any time.

Question 6 again emphasises that all such charts are approximate. The answer to parts (c) and (d) can be given over a wide acceptable range.

1. a) Italy   b) July

     c) i) May   ii) September

2. a) about 11 °F   b) 8 °F

3. a) 6 °F   b) 7 °F

4. a) Morocco in August   b) Either resort in July

5. a) August, April   b) August, April

6. a) i) $2\frac{1}{2}$ ii) 4   iii) 1

     b) i) 25 °F   ii) 26 °F

     c) about 170   d) about 46

7. a) 25 °F   b) 22 °F

EXERCISE 2g   An interesting discussion on the International Date line can be introduced if it is felt to be appropriate. The problem of jet-lag can also give rise to interesting comments.

1. a) 11 a.m.   b) 2 a.m.

2. a) 2.30 a.m.   b) 10.30 a.m.

3. a) 11 a.m.   b) 6 p.m.

4. a) 2 p.m.   b) 4 a.m.

5. a) 03.10   b) 9 hours forward   c) 3 a.m.

6. a) i) noon   ii) 9 p.m.   iii) 7 p.m.   b) 1 p.m. to 5 p.m.

CHAPTER 3   **Travel Graphs** ▬▬▬▬▬▬▬▬▬▬▬▬▬▬▬▬▬

For some pupils this chapter may be their first study of Travel Graphs. Those who followed the topic in Book 2 will probably not spend too much time on the early exercises. These are, however, important, for so much depends on a thorough understanding of the basics before the graphs and later exercises can be tackled satisfactorily.

EXERCISE 3a   This exercise can profitably be used for oral work.

1. a) 250 miles	b) 25 miles	
2. a) 28 km	b) 98 km	c) 14 km
3. a) 2700 miles	b) 450 miles	c) 200 miles
4. a) 60 km	b) 35 km	c) 25 km
5. a) $1\frac{1}{2}$ hrs	b) 45 min	
6. a) 35 miles	b) 28 miles	
7. a) 1.2 s	b) 2.6 s	

8. 40 km/h	**13.** 11 m/s	**18.** 300 m.p.h
9. 8 m/s	**14.** 120 km/h	**19.** 400 m.p.h.
10. 90 m.p.h.	**15.** 75 m.p.h.	**20.** 500 m.p.h.
11. 80 km/h	**16.** 550 m.p.h.	
12. 72 m.p.h.	**17.** 300 m.p.h.	

EXERCISE 3b   Many simple examples of average speed should be used to introduce the idea. Use well known local bus routes, train journeys, and car trips, for additional oral examples.

The successful solution of questions 6 to 10 will indicate a clear understanding of average speed. A local OS map should provide several examples similar to question 12.

1.

	Distance in miles	Speed in m.p.h.	Time in hours
First part of journey	60	15	4
Second part of journey	36	18	2
Whole journey	96	16	6

2.

	Distance in kilometres	Speed in km/h	Time in hours
First part of journey	100	50	2
Second part of journey	120	40	3
Whole journey	220	44	5

3.

	Distance in miles	Speed in m.p.h.	Time in hours
First part of journey	20	8	$2\frac{1}{2}$
Second part of journey	18	12	$1\frac{1}{2}$
Whole journey	38	9.5	4

4.

	Distance in kilometres	Speed in km/h	Time in hours
First part of journey	300	60	5
Resting period	–	–	1
Second part of journey	200	50	4
Whole journey	500	50	10

5.

	Distance in miles	Speed in m.p.h.	Time in hours
First part of journey	80	60	$1\frac{1}{3}$
Resting period	–	–	$\frac{5}{12}$ $\frac{1}{6}$
Second part of journey	70	35	2
Whole journey	150	~~40~~	$3\frac{3}{4}$ $3\frac{1}{2}$

$42\frac{6}{7}$

6.

	Distance in km	Speed in km/h	Time in hours
First part of journey	30	45	$\frac{2}{3}$
Second part of journey	130	65	2
Third part of journey	40	30	$1\frac{1}{3}$
Whole journey	200	50	4

7.

	Distance in miles	Speed in m.p.h.	Time in hours
First part of journey	120	48	$2\frac{1}{2}$
Resting period	–	–	$\frac{1}{4}$
Second part of journey	180	72	$2\frac{1}{2}$
Resting period	–	–	$\frac{1}{2}$
Third part of journey	50	40	$1\frac{1}{4}$
Whole journey	350	50	7

8. 8 m.p.h.
9. $8\frac{2}{5}$ m.p.h.
10. 16 km/h
11. a) 1 h 42 min   b) 2 h 35 min
12.

	Distance in km	Speed in km/h	Time in hours	Order of arrival
Pedestrian	6	6	1	Second
Cyclist	18	12	$1\frac{1}{2}$	Third
Motorist	27	36	$\frac{3}{4}$	First

EXERCISE 3c   Use this exercise for oral work in class.

1. a) 60 km   b) 3 h   c) 20 km/h
2. a) 20 miles   b) $1\frac{1}{2}$ h   c) $13\frac{1}{3}$ m.p.h.
3. a) 40 miles   b) 5 h   c) 8 m.p.h.
4. a) 160 km   b) 2.3 h   c) 70 km/h

EXERCISE 3d   A simple, yet important, introductory exercise to the drawing of travel graphs.

1.

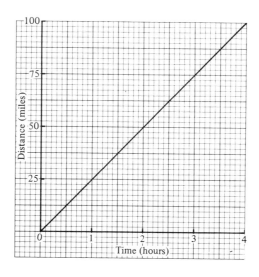

2.

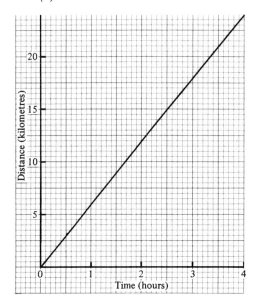

5.

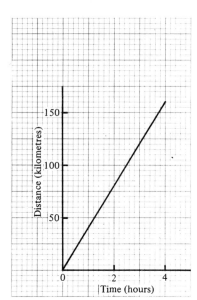

3.

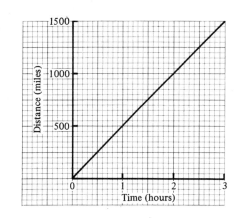

6.

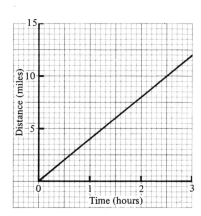

4.

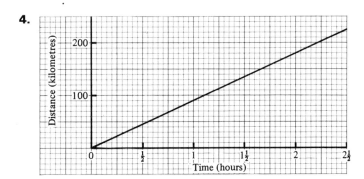

7.

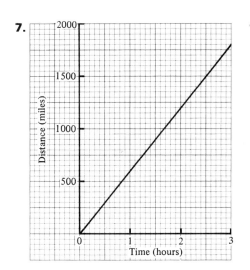

10.

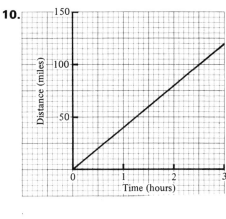

8.

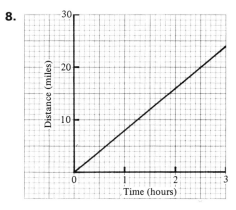

11.

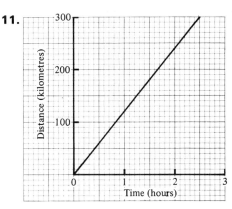

9.

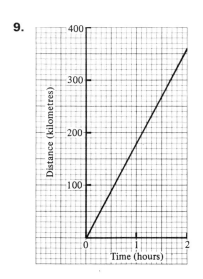

12.

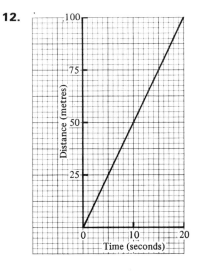

13. a) $\frac{1}{2}$ hour   b) i) 90 km   ii) 45 km
14. a) 20 miles   b) $1\frac{1}{4}$ hours

EXERCISE 3e   In questions 1 and 2 point out that an increase in gradient signifies an increase in speed. The remaining questions attempt to lead pupils through the problem one step at a time.

1. a) 90 m, 30 m/s   b) 80 m, 16 m/s   c) i) 5 m/s   ii) 2 m/s
2. a) true   b) false   c) true   d) false   e) true
3. a) i) 80 miles   ii) 70 miles   b) i) 15.30   ii) 16.30
    c) 80 miles   d) $1\frac{7}{8}$ hours
4. a) 30 km, $1\frac{1}{2}$ h   b) i) $\frac{1}{2}$ h   ii) $\frac{1}{2}$ h   c) Yes   d) 20 km/h
    e) i) 60 km   ii) 15 km/h
    f) A speed of 20 km/h suggests that she travelled on her bicycle.
5. a) 2 h   b) 10.15, 13.15   c) coach 80 km/h, car 120 km/h
    d) 60 km/h   e) $1\frac{3}{4}$ h
6. a) i) 9.08, 10.38   ii) 1 h 30 min   iii) 150 miles   iv) $112\frac{1}{2}$ m.p.h.
    v) 1 h 52 min   vi) 80 m.p.h. approx.
    b) i) 56 miles   ii) 94 miles   c) i) 2 min   ii) 50 min
7. a) 10 min   b) 8 km
    c) Yes (the gradient is steepest for the second part of the journey).
    d) less   e) 3 km   f) 13.10 M/NS
8. a) i) 30 miles, 36 miles, 56 miles   ii) 45 ~~miles~~, 30 miles   iii) 40 m.p.h.
    iv) 48 m.p.h.   v) 35 min   vi) 32 m.p.h.   vii) 29 m.p.h. (approx)
    b) ~~twice~~   c) no   d) Ron, $\frac{1}{2}$ h   e) 8.40
          three
          times

EXERCISE 3f   In this exercise travel graphs have to be drawn before the questions can be answered. Pupils who complete these questions satisfactorily show a fairly sound understanding of travel graphs. (Note that graphs are drawn to $\frac{1}{4}$ scale.)

1. a) B 35 miles, C 60 miles, D 100 miles
    b) i) 70 m.p.h. ii) $44\frac{1}{2}$ m.p.h. iii) $68\frac{1}{2}$ m.p.h. iv) $55\frac{1}{2}$ m.p.h. (approx)
    c) 5 min   d) 1.10   e) 13.57   f) 62 miles from A at 1.17
    g) 33 miles

2.

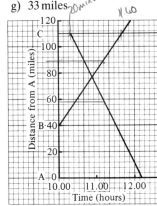

    a) 11.40
        56 m.p.h.
    b) 38 miles
        28 miles
    c) 1 h 59 min
    d) $\dfrac{110}{\frac{59}{60}} = 55\frac{1}{2}$ Mph
    e) 31 miles.

3.

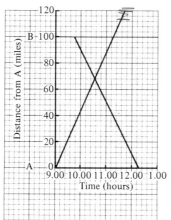

4. a) and b)

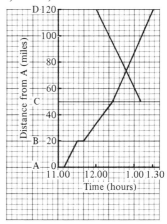

a) 40 m.p.h.
b) at approx 10.32,
   69 miles from A
c) 40 miles

c) i) 12.24
   ii) 70 m.p.h.
   iii) 1.10
   iv) 46 miles from D at 12.46
   v) 33 miles from A

5.

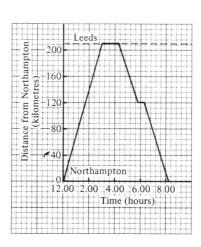

a) 70 km/h
b) 8.15

6.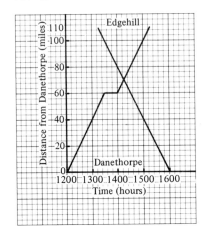

a) 13.30
b) 15.15
c) 40 m.p.h.
d) 70 miles from Danethorpe at 14.15

CHAPTER 4   Circles, Solids and Nets

These exercises revise and consolidate work on the construction and on the mensuration of circles and solids. Some pupils find 3-D work surprisingly difficult and it is recommended that as many nets as possible are made by the pupils and kept for future reference. In some cases it is sensible not to stick the edges, so that the 'solids' can be opened out. Clear plastic solids and wire models (as long as they are stiff enough) are also useful.

EXERCISE 4a

1. a) 6 cm   b) 2.4 cm   c) 0.6 m   d) 82 cm
2. a) 4.5 cm   b) 1.3 m   c) 0.43 m   d) 31 cm
3. a) 17 cm   b) 195 cm   c) 5.34 m   d) 66.6 cm
4. a) 12 cm   b) 7.8 m   c) 2.4 m   d) 30 cm
5. a) 44.0 cm   b) 68.5 cm   c) 4.14 m   d) 2.39 m
6. a) 84.95 cm^2 b) 28.3 cm^2 c) 154 cm^2 d) 27 cm^2
7. 54.7 cm, 238 cm^2
8. 126 cm^2

EXERCISE 4b

1. 226 cm^3
2. 0.088 m^3
3. 2000 cm^3
4. 12 000 cm^3
5. 1360 cm^3
6. 25 100 cm^3
7. 931 × 10^3 cm^3
8. 196 cm^3 (196 × 10^3 mm^3)
9. 169 × 10^3 cm^3; 132 × 10^3 cm^3
10. 1920 cm^3
11. 94.5 cm^3
12. 102 × 10^2 cm^3
13. 13 cm
14. 16 cm
15. 251 cm^3, 127 (or 128 if π is cancelled)

EXERCISE 4c
1. C and G
2. JI
3. 6
4. 12
5. 8
6. square
7. 36 cm²
8. 216 cm²

9.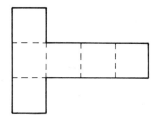

EXERCISE 4d
1. a) 8 cm³   b) 27 cm³   c) 0.001 m³ (10³ cm³)
2. 115 740
3. 64 cm³
4. 576 cm³
5. 0.139 m³

EXERCISE 4e
1. M and E
2. LK
3. 6
4. 12
5. 8
6. rectangular
7. two are 35 cm², two are 21 cm², two are 15 cm²
8. 142 cm²
9.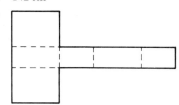

EXERCISE 4f   Two pieces of extended work suggest themselves at this point: (a) investigation of which nets to draw for a given box to give the most efficient use of card when several have to be cut, (b) investigation of the relationship between volume and surface area, e.g. for a box of given volume (say 360 cm³), what dimensions give the smallest surface area?

1. 18 cm³
2. 2 cm
3. 7 cm
4. 10 800 cm³ (0.0108 m³)
5. 0.33 m
6. 8.62 (to 3 s.f.)
7. 2074 cm³
8. cuboid 78.4 cm³, cylinder 86.0 cm³, cube 97.3 cm³
9. 56 cm³
10. 840 cm³

EXERCISE 4g
1. J and D
2. G and I
3. 9
4. 6
5. 5
6. 3
7. triangular

8.

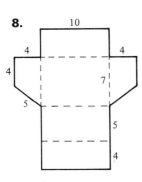

9.

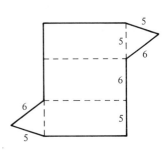

a) 4 cm   b) 12 cm²
c) one is 72 cm², two are 60 cm²
d) 216 cm²

10.

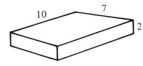

any cuboid net; cuboid; 208 cm²

11. a)   i) F   ii) J
            iii) D
      b)   i) IJ   ii) GH
            iii) DE
      c) 5 cm
      d) 72 cm²

EXERCISE 4h
1. 94 cm³
2. 56 cm³
3. 88.8 cm³
4. 1005 cm³
5. 3750 cm³
6. a) 9.62 cm²
7. a) 1.5 m²
8. a) 84 cm³

b) 72.375 kg
b) 19 200 cm³   c) 148 kg
b) 7.5 m³   c) 12.5 m²
b) 2827 mm³   c) 29

EXERCISE 4i
2. 5
3. 5
4. 8
5. 4

6.

7. a) hollow cylinder with no ends
      b)

8. cone

EXERCISE 4j **2.** a) cuboid

b) cone

c) triangular prism

d) tetrahedron

3. a) and c)

4. a) (i)

5.

triangular prism

6. a) A, C, E, G

b) square pyramid

c) i) 5   ii) 8

EXERCISE 4k In question 6, some small cubes (children's building blocks, Oxo or sugar cubes) are useful.

1. a) 88 cm   b) 616 cm²

2. a) 0.293 m³ (292 800 cm³)   b) 1415 cm³   c) 3035 cm³

3. a) square pyramid   b) cone with-base

4. a) 8   b) 5   c) 5

5. a) 6 cm × 6 cm × 2 cm   b) 72 cm³   c) 16 cm²

6. a) 24   b) 20   c) We do not know the shape at the back; 9; 12.

7. a) square pyramid   b) i) 5   ii) 8   iii) 5   c) 12 cm   d) 340 cm²

EXERCISE 4l **1.** a) 35.2 cm   b) 98.5 cm²

2. 2772 cm³

3. a) triangular prism

b) 5 cm

c) 48 cm³

d)

e) 108 cm²

4. a) 4   b) 6   c) 4

5. a) 22 cm   b) 38½ cm²

c) 539 cm³

d) 385 cm²;

    x = 14 cm, y = 22 cm

6. a)

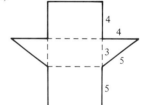

b) J

c) B, G and I

d) triangular prism

e) 6 cm²

f) 36 cm³

7. a) i) A and B

ii) B and D, D and E

b) 8, 12, 18

c) A, B and C; A, B and D;

    B, C and E

EXERCISE 4m   **1.** A   **2.** A   **3.** C   **4.** B   **5.** D   **6.** C   **7.** C

CHAPTER 5   Sections and Symmetry ▬▬▬▬▬▬▬▬▬▬

Solids made for Chapter 4 will be useful. Objects made from material which can be sliced will help many pupils. Polystyrene (blocks from packaging) is a good material to use, but it does need a sharp thin instrument, such as a scalpel, to cut it. Modelling clay and 'Play-doh' are also useful.

EXERCISE 5a   **1.**

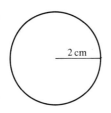

2.

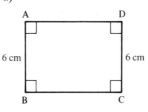

3. a) equilateral
    b) triangular pyramid
       or tetrahedron

4. a) equilateral
    b) triangular pyramid
    c) i) 7   ii) 12   iii) 7
    d) 8

5. a)

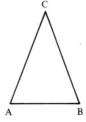

      no

    b) rectangle

6. the cut in question 5

7.

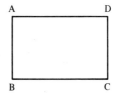

    a) rectangle
    b) CD, BC, BD, BE

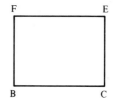

    c) no, because BF is longer than BA

8.

    a) isosceles
    b) AC is shorter than 9 cm.

9.

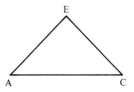

a) isosceles
b) AC is longer than AB.

10.

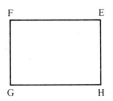

a) rectangle
b) FG is shorter than FB.

11.

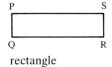

rectangle

12. a)

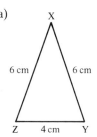

b) The section is the same shape as △ABF.

13. a)

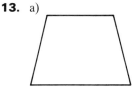

b)

c)

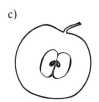

EXERCISE 5b

1. yes		**6.** no	
2. no		**7.** yes	
3. yes		**8.** yes	
4. yes		**9.** yes	
5. yes		**10.** no	

EXERCISE 5c

1. 1	**3.** infinite	**5.** 3
2. 2	**4.** 4	**6.** 9

EXERCISE 5d   **1.** a) 8   b) 5   c) 5   **4.** a) 2

2. a) 2   b) 10   b)

3.

5. infinite

EXERCISE 5e   **1.** A   **2.** C   **3.** D   **4.** A   **5.** C

CHAPTER 6   Formulae

A discussion of the tendency to abbreviate names, etc., into initials (e.g. BBC, ITV, ICI, DHSS) and the reasons for doing so, can usefully lead on to a discussion of the sensible abbreviations of a set of instructions for finding a given quantity, i.e., a formula. Known formulae, such as $C = 2\pi r$, can be used as examples. Write it out in full using no symbols and discuss why we abbreviate it.

EXERCISE 6a   **1.** 22   **4.** a) 217   b) 24.96
                   2. a) 25   b) 48   **5.** a) 4   b) 6
                   3. a) 11   b) −14   **6.** a) 8   b) 3.1

7. a) 100   b) £235
8. a) $x = 17, y = 3$ b) £1.70
9. a) 8   b) 26
10. a) £38   b) £62.50
11. a) 21   b) 234
12. a) £24   b) £1080

13. D   **14.** B   **15.** C

EXERCISE 6b   **1.** a) 13   b) $y = x + 4$
                   2. a) £2.40   b) $C = 40n$
                   3. a) 150 miles   b) $d = 50t$
                   4. a) 15   b) $R = 2x + 3$
                   5. a) 25   b) $N = x + 5$ c) $M = 2x$
                   6. a) 19   b) $N = 3p + 1$
                   7. a) 15 cm   b) $p = a + b + c$

8. C   **10.** D   **12.** C
9. B   **11.** D

EXERCISE 6c   **1.** 12   **5.** 12   **9.** 4
                   2. 16   **6.** 2   **10.** $3\frac{1}{2}$
                   3. 9   **7.** 2   **11.** 4
                   4. 3   **8.** 8   **12.** 2

13. B   **14.** D   **15.** A   **16.** B   **17.** B

EXERCISE 6d   **1.** $q = p - r$ **5.** $m = l + 4$
2. $h = g - 7$ **6.** $q = p + r$
3. $B = A - 3C$ **7.** $z = x + 5y$
4. $b = y - 2a$ **8.** $b = a + cd$

9. $a = \dfrac{F}{m}$ **13.** $n = 6m$

10. $q = \dfrac{p}{8}$ **14.** $z = 5y$

11. $x = \dfrac{y^2}{4a}$ **15.** $q = pr$

12. $r = \dfrac{C}{2\pi}$ **16.** $F = \mu N$

17. $T = \dfrac{D}{s}$ **22.** $h = \dfrac{A}{b}$

18. $c = y - mx$ **23.** $x = y + 5$

19. $a = p - b - c$ **24.** $\pi = \dfrac{C}{2r}$

20. $R = \dfrac{E}{i^2}$ **25.** $\pi = \dfrac{A}{r^2}$

21. $x = \dfrac{y}{m}$

26. C   **27.** A   **28.** D   **29.** D   **30.** B

EXERCISE 6e   **1.** a) 19   b) 13.2   c) 4   d) $y = c - 2x$ e) 9
2. a) 13   b) 7   c) 4   d) $b = P - 2a$ e) 7   f) $a = \frac{1}{2}(P - b)$
3. a) $10\frac{1}{2}$ b) 5.4   c) 9   d) $a = 2s - b - c$ e) 5

EXERCISE 6f   **1.** $a = 9 - c$ **5.** $x = \frac{1}{2}(y - z)$
2. $x = 4 - s$ **6.** $a = \frac{1}{2}(b + c)$
3. $P = 100 - Q$ **7.** $b = \frac{1}{2}(P - 2l)$
4. $k = m - h$ **8.** $b = \frac{1}{3}(x - 5a)$

9. $x = \dfrac{y - c}{m}$ **13.** $b = \dfrac{a + c}{3}$ or $b = \frac{1}{3}(a + c)$

10. $a = \dfrac{P - 2b}{2}$ or $\frac{1}{2}(P - 2b)$ **14.** $y = x + 4$

11. $c = 3b - a$ **15.** $b = \dfrac{P - 2a}{2}$ or $\frac{1}{2}(P - 2a)$

12. $x = y - 4$ **16.** $k = mh - y$

17. A   **18.** C   **19.** D   **20.** C

EXERCISE 6g
1. $a = 4c$
2. $y = 3x$
3. $r = \dfrac{4}{P}$
4. $z = aw$
5. $b = 12a$

6. $x = 2y - 6$
7. $q = 2p - 3$
8. $b = 2a - c$
9. $y = \frac{1}{2}(9x - 6)$ or $\frac{3}{2}(3x - 2)$
10. $y = 4x - 12$

EXERCISE 6h
1. 15
2. 8

3. $z = x + y$
4. $452\,\text{cm}^2$

5. $t = 40M + 30$
6. $b = \frac{1}{2}(p - a)$

EXERCISE 6j
1. 4
2. $4\frac{1}{2}$

3. $b = \frac{1}{3}(a - c)$
4. £92

5. $C = 6y + x$
6. $z = \dfrac{y}{x}$

EXERCISE 6k
1. D   2. B   3. C   4. D   5. A

CHAPTER 7   Working with Percentages

The basic percentage processes are revised in the first exercise, but after that the emphasis is on the use of percentages in everyday contexts. Discuss why percentages are used: for example show pupils a sales advertisement which includes wording such as 'Massive 20% reductions on m.r.p. on selected items'. Ask why it is presented this way and not as a list of reductions on some of the goods.

EXERCISE 7a

	Percentage	Fraction	Decimal
1.	20%	$\frac{1}{5}$	0.2
2.	50%	$\frac{1}{2}$	0.5
3.	10%	$\frac{1}{10}$	0.1
4.	12%	$\frac{3}{25}$	0.12
5.	25%	$\frac{1}{4}$	0.25
6.	60%	$\frac{3}{5}$	0.6
7.	12.5%	$\frac{1}{8}$	0.125
8.	35%	$\frac{7}{20}$	0.35
9.	75%	$\frac{3}{4}$	0.75
10.	40%	$\frac{2}{5}$	0.4
11.	15%	$\frac{3}{20}$	0.15
12.	6%	$\frac{3}{50}$	0.06
13.	32%	$\frac{8}{25}$	0.32
14.	150%	$1\frac{1}{2}$	1.5
15.	102%	$1\frac{1}{50}$	1.02
16.	21.5%	$\frac{43}{200}$	0.215
17.	1.5%	$\frac{3}{200}$	0.015
18.	$7\frac{1}{2}\%$	$\frac{3}{40}$	0.075
19.	17.5%	$\frac{4}{15}$	0.175
20.	120%	$1\frac{1}{5}$	1.2

EXERCISE 7b Question 8 brings in VAT for the first time. Answers involving calculation of VAT are given correct to the nearest penny but in practice VAT is rounded down.

1. £3.60
2. 3p
3. 0.27 m or 27 cm
4. 15 cm
5. £9.60

6. £48
7. £3.15
8. 78p
9. £16.70
10. £51

EXERCISE 7c
1. 15%
2. 80%
3. 60%
4. 20%
5. 4%
6. 25%
7. 90%
8. 5%

9. 20%
10. 63%
11. 20%
12. 6%
13. 37.5%
14. 16.7% to 1 d.p.
15. 25%

EXERCISE 7d
1. 51p
2. £2.95
3. £25
4. £7.50
5. 20%
6. 10%
7. $33\frac{1}{3}$%
8. 25%
9. shop A by 4p
10. a) 6 cm   b) 36 cm²   c) 125%

EXERCISE 7e
1. £225
2. £96
3. £1000
4. 8 cm
5. 1.9 m

6. £2.07
7. £190.40
8. £2.65
9. £126
10. 39 cm by 65 cm

EXERCISE 7f Question 12 arose from actual experience. One of the authors bought two such items and the assistant insisted on giving a 20% reduction because two were bought. This can form the basis of a discussion, including the assistant's prospects of continued employment and what would have happened if ten items had been bought!

1. £195
2. £140.40

3.

	£
10 brackets at £1.50 each	15.00
2 uprights at £6.00 each	12.00
total	27.00
VAT at 15%	4.05
to pay	<u>31.05</u>

4. 68%

5. 30%

6. a) 200 m²   b) 144 m²   c) 72%

7. 25%

8. £127.50

9. £1200

10. store A by £2.90

11. £36

12. a) 40   b) 25%

13. £75, 50%

14. £1110

15. a) 127 500   b) 153 000

16. a) 50   b) 40%   c) 30%

17. a) 9   b) 11   c) 22%

18. a) £44 000   b) £48 400

19. a) £450   b) £405

20.

	£
2 bags cement	15.00
30 paving stones	60.00
	75.00
2% trade discount	1.50
	73.50
VAT at 15%	11.03
	<u>84.53</u>

EXERCISE 7g
1. D
2. B
3. C
4. B
5. A
6. A
7. C
8. B
9. D

CHAPTER 8   Borrowing Money ▬▬▬▬▬▬▬▬▬▬▬▬▬▬

The text and exercises may give the impression that getting a mortgage, a bank loan, etc.is a simple procedure. Advertising policy tends to confirm this. It can come as a shock to many people to find that it is not just a case of walking in and asking for a loan. Some investigatory work on conditions for obtaining credit is a good idea.

EXERCISE 8a
1. £420
2. £304
3. £159.30
4. £292
5. a) £364.50   b) £4374   c) £109 350
6. a) £23 750   b) £1250
7. a) £37 800   b) 4200
8. a) £42 000   b) £512.40

EXERCISE 8b
1. £660
2. £974.40, £2923.20
3. a) £19   b) £842.40   c) £258.88

EXERCISE 8c Hire purchase as such is not now a very common form of credit. Large items, such as cars, are often financed by leasing arrangements where a small extra payment on the last leasing payment actually purchases the car. It is sensible to point out the variety of forms of credit (without going into details) and the necessity to read such agreements carefully.

1. £956, £136
2. a) £15   b) £64.50
3. £128
4. a) £170   b) £1079
5. a) £62.50   b) £268.78   c) £18.78
6. a) £10 129.68   b) £9500.10
7. a) £427.50   b) £528   c) £100.50
8. a) £2250   b) £3910.80
9. a) £804.30   b) 15%
10. a) £250   b) £900   c) £75

EXERCISE 8d
1. £6.23
2. £5
3. £17.50
4. No, he will be £72.50 over his credit limit.
5. a) £60   b) £450
6. No, it will take me £30 over my credit limit.
7. balance £216, yes

EXERCISE 8e

1. £114
2. £17.50
3. £22.50
4. £3.75
5. £120

6. a) £27.30   b) £25.35   c) £35
7. a) £250   b) £50
8. a) £84   b) £70   c) £122.50
9. a) £63.75   b) the piano
10. a) £112   b) £109.76

EXERCISE 8f

1. £180
2. £332.50
3. £90
4. a) £105   b) £60

5.

	£	£
Gross premium		250
40% no claims bonus	100	
5% reduction for excess	12.50	
Renewal premium		137.50

6. a) £900   b) £17.31
7. a) £836   b) £16.08
8. £93.50
9. a) £360   b) £270   c) £180
10. £98.70

EXERCISE 8g

1. £274
2. £24 000
3. £3139.20
4. £1016
5. a) £110
   b) £464
6. £44
7. £3.75
8. £105

9.

A & B Builders Merchants

	£
10 m of 15 mm copper tube at 80 p per m	8.00
1 × 5 mm stopcock	2.75
	10.75
5% discount	0.54
	10.21
VAT at 15%	1.53
Total	11.74

10.

	£
Capital depreciation	500.00
Road tax	100.00
Insurance: gross premium £250	
Less 60% no claims bonus £150	100.00
Service	150.00
Petrol: 800 litres at 40 p per litre	320.00
	1170.00

CHAPTER 9   Personal Finance

It would be most profitable to spend a little time in general discussion of the topics raised in this chapter. The provision by pupils of real life examples of such things as wages slips, building society pass books etc should be encouraged (but with caution over confidentiality). Most building societies are only too pleased to give pupils copies of their many leaflets.

EXERCISE 9a   Actual wages may be calculated using the information available at the local Employment Centre or in newspapers. Get pupils to guess what the take-home pay will be for various gross pays. Most pupils have no idea of the amount deducted from the average pay packet. It is quite easy to extend the discussion into 'What are deductions, such as NIC, superannuation and income tax, made for?' and 'Are they fair to everybody?' Perhaps an actual clocking-in card or pay slip could be acquired.

1. £140
2. £171
3. £112.50
4. £247.50
5. £183.75
6. £4, £5, £27.50
7. a) 7 a.m.   b) 3.30 p.m.   c) 1 h
   d) i) 5 h   ii) $2\frac{1}{2}$ h
   e) Thursday   f) $37\frac{1}{2}$ h   g) £150
8. 36 hours, £9.52, £90.44
9. a) £147   b) £6.30   c) £175.50   d) £9
   e) Arthur
10. a) 7.30 a.m.   b) yes Friday   c) 7 h   d) 1 h
    e) 3.30 p.m.   f) Thursday   g) Wednesday and Saturday
    h) 6 hours   i) Thursday   j) £156.60
11. £3.60, £5.40, £196.20

EXERCISE 9b   Some questions that could be raised in discussion are: Why are some workers paid commission? Could all workers be paid in this way? Can you name some jobs that cannot be paid in this way? What are the advantages/disadvantages of being paid commission?

1. a)£250   b) £162.50   5. £159.50
2. £440   6. £143
3. £187.50   7. £162.50
4. £112   8. £360

EXERCISE 9c   1. a) 1125   b) 500   c) 625   d) £125

2.

	a)	b) i)	b) ii)	c)
Ms Arnold	186	100	86	£100.90
Mr Beynon	158	80	78	£86.70
Miss Capstrek	194	100	94	£106.10
Mr Davis	225	100	125	£126.25
Mrs Edmunds	191	100	91	£104.15

d) Thursday

3.

	a)	b) i)	ii)	b) iii)
John Aitkin	743	£90	£58.32	£148.32
Edna Owen	716	£90	£51.84	£141.84
Mair Price	751	£90	£60.24	£150.24
Len Brown	742	£90	£58.08	£148.08
Helen Peters	748	£90	£59.52	£149.52

c) Mair Price, Helen Peters, John Aitkin, Len Brown, Edna Owen
d) i) Wednesday ii) Monday
4. a) 255   b) 17
5. £53.72

EXERCISE 9d Sharpen up pupils' mental arithmetic facility by giving an annual salary and asking for an estimate of the weekly salary. Suggest short cut methods where appropriate, e.g. £8000 p.a. is approximately £160 per week (Divide the £8000 by 100 and double.) A calculator confirms the result. In this case the exact value, correct to the nearest whole number, is £154.

1. a) £550   b) £126.92
2. a) £742   b) 171.23
3. a) £637.50   b) £147.12
4. a) £1231   b) £284.08
5. a) £1861.25   b) £429.52
6. £7848
7. £10 080
8. £13 632
9. £5904
10. £18 864

EXERCISE 9e Discuss percentage wage/salary increases and whether or not pupils consider them to be fair. Also inflation and its effect on wages. Cite simple cases where inflation is low (4%) but wage increases slightly higher (5%), as against high inflation (25%) and wage rises that are high (20%) but which are lower than the rate of inflation. Which is preferred? How many understand that prices continue to go up when the rate of inflation falls?

1. a) £16   b) £96   **3.** a) £15.60   b) £145.60
2. a) £8.50   b) £93.50   **4.** a) £12   b) £162

5. a) £12	b) £212	**9.** a) £9.80	b) £289.80
6. a) £12.75	b) £182.75	**10.** a) £40.80	b) £380.80
7. a) £5.80	b) £150.80	**11.** 12% increase	
8. a) £10	b) £210	**12.** £16 per week	

EXERCISE 9f Do we get value for money for our National Insurance Contributions? What do they pay for? Should we all pay more (less) for better (poorer) services?

1. £2.85	**7.** £38.69	**13.** £5.80
2. £3.50	**8.** £2.30	**14.** £86.50
3. £6.80	**9.** £6.45	**15.** £4.75
4. £62.09	**10.** £15	**16.** £4.48
5. £80	**11.** £20.40	**17.** £5.20
6. £57.59	**12.** £3.84	**18.** £97.21

EXERCISE 9g Income Tax was introduced by William Pitt in 1798 as a temporary tax to meet war expenses. Apart from the period 1816–42 it has been with us ever since. Is it a fair way of collecting the money required by the government to run the country? Can you think of better, fairer ways of raising the same sum?

Investigate the present level of taxation, including the different rates for the different bands. Are taxes higher/lower today than they were a) 5 years ago, b) 10 years ago, c) 20 years ago?

1.

Name	Gross income	Allowances	Taxable income
J. Peters	£9000	£2500	£6500
E. John	£8151	£1730	£6421
P. Brown	£15 430	£3784	£11 646
M. Jacob	£24 380	£4530	£19 850
A. Khan	£12 995	£4731	£8264
C. White	£12 670	£3233	£9437

2. a) £1950, £1926.30, £3493.80, £5955, £2479.20, £2831.10
b) £1820, £1797.88, £3260.88, £5558, £2313.92, £2642.36

3.

Name	Gross pay per calendar month	Annual allowances	Annual taxable income
R. Lee	£324	£1200	£2688
M. Davis	£640	£2240	£5440
S. Axe	£468	£2970	£2646
J. Brewer	£836	£4320	£5712
E. Evans	£1200	£3600	£10 800

4. a) £806.40, £1632, £793.80, £1713.60, £3240
     b) £67.20, £136, £66.15, £142.80, £270

5.

Name	Gross weekly pay	Annual non taxable allowances	Gross annual income	Annual taxable income	Weekly income tax payment	Weekly income net of income tax
S. Wilcox	£100	£4200	£5200	£1000	£5.77	£94.23
E. Cole	£130	£3945	£6760	£2815	£16.24	£113.76
I. Tucker	£170	£4536	£8840	£4304	£24.83	£145.17
J. Parry	£185	£2674	£9620	£6946	£40.07	£144.93
P. Lewis	£240	£4333	£12 480	£8147	£47.00	£193.00
C. Snook	£350	£3780	£18 200	£14 420	£83.19	£266.81

EXERCISE 9h   Some introductory work which is suitable here should have been done at the beginning of the chapter. This exercise brings home to pupils just how high a percentage of a person's gross wage the wage earner never sees because of deductions at source.

	Employee	Gross pay	Deductions			Net pay
			NIC	Income tax	Person fund	
1.	Aitken	£95				£69.85
2.	Conti	£110				£74.66
3.	Daley	£145				£96.75
4.	Griffin	£176				£117.20
5.	Hall	£132				£88.70
6.	Jones	£204				£133.24
7.	Kelly	£86				£63.84
8.	O'Keefe	£183	£16.47			
9.	Ryton	£313			£18.78	
10.	Villiers	£242		£48.72		

11. £119.14
12. £114.94
13. £203.80

EXERCISE 9i Stress the importance of saving, and the fact that far greater effort is required to save than to spend.

1. £852.81
2. a) £102.81   b) £546.54   c) £549.64
3. £320 on 16 August
4. £750 on 10 August
5. £148.98, interest is added to the balance
6. 10, £1865
7. a) 6   b) 3
8. £50.74 from 15 October to 30 November
9. £39.41
10. £927.88
11. £1200
12.

Date	Cashier's initials	Description	Withdrawn	Invested	Balance
		Balance brought forward			461.22
9 Jan 87	WEA	CHEQUE		64.58	525.80
15 Jan 87	WEA	CASH	100		425.80
29 Jan 87	WEA	CHEQUE		374.43	800.23
3 Feb 87	WEA	CASH	250		550.23
21 Feb 87	WEA	CHEQUE	280		270.23
28 Feb 87	WEA	CHEQUE		173.80	444.03
3 March 87	WEA	CASH	180		264.03
25 March 87	WEA	CASH	230		34.03

13. £34.03

EXERCISE 9j Most pupils have heard of National Savings Certificates and will be receptive to more detailed information about them. Show pupils the real thing, and encourage them to obtain the relevant leaflets from the post office so that the appreciation of given certificates can be indicated clearly.

1. 4
2. 18
3. £225
4. £3750
5. £912
6. £1821.60
7. a) £875 b) £1276.80 c) £401.80
8. £182.40
9. £574
10. £243.60
11. £918.40
12. a) 75   b) £1875 c) £861
13. a) 44   b) £1100 c) £237.60

EXERCISE 9k   1. D   2. C   3. A   4. C   5. B

CHAPTER 10 Household Expenses

This is an ideal chapter for using actual bills. Check the various calculations. Their use will provide many discussion points and be of value to everybody after they have left school.

EXERCISE 10a It should be stressed that the number of units used is the *difference* between the meter reading at the end and beginning of the quarter. Many pupils have other ideas! Discuss the need for a standing charge. Stress that electric heating is expensive whereas lighting from electricity is cheap. There are however special tariffs, such as Economy 7, which encourage the use of electricity when more is produced than is required. The cost is usually about half the normal rate.

Some ideas for investigation work are:
1. Compare a) the installation costs, b) the running costs, of heating your home using electricity, gas, oil or solid fuel. Would you expect the answer to be the same for houses of different sizes?
2. Gas boards operate a Budget plan. How does this work? Why do many householders prefer to use this method of payment?
3. Which of the four fuels referred to above do you think is best for your home assuming that costs do not matter? Consider such things as cleanliness, storage, the time spent in operating the system, safety aspects, etc.

1. 244

2. 1259

3. 1187

4. 2108

5. 797

6. 573

7. 1858

8. 420

9. 1612

10.

First quarter	854
Second quarter	512
Third quarter	364
Fourth quarter	1254

11. 838
403
385
1208

12.

Date	Meter Reading	Number of units used in the specified quarter
10 January	53 498	
7 April	54 410	First: 912
13 July	54 856	Second: 446
9 October	55 450	Third: 594
12 January	56 634	Fourth: 1184

13.

Date	Meter Reading	Number of units used in the specified quarter
5 March	16 955	
12 June	17 394	First: 439
10 September	17 791	Second: 397
6 December	18 636	Third: 845
8 March	19 914	Fourth: 1278

14. £105.82
15. £91.20
16. £133.28
17. £113.41
18. £82.93
19. £122.37
20. £41.49
21. £321.79

22. £135
23. £163
24. £120.50
25. £91.86
26. £286.36
27. 594
28. £10.54

29.

Appliance	Rating	Number of hours used in the week	Number of units used	Cost at 8.45 p per unit
Cooker	8 kW	5	40	3.38
TV set	250 W	36	9	0.76
Hi fi	100 W	6	0.6	0.05
Refrigerator	200 W	50	10	0.85
Washing Machine	2 kW	5	10	0.85
Electric fire	3 kW	18	54	4.56
Vacuum cleaner	500 W	2	1	0.08
6 Light bulbs	100 W (each)	40 (each)	4	0.34

£151.16

EXERCISE 10b The calorific value of gas, and its two values (i.e. around 1035 for natural gas, and half this value for town gas) is given more by way of interest than as knowledge required for examination purposes.

1. 132
2. 171
3. 116
4. 324

5.

Date	Meter reading	Number of units used in quarter
3 January	003 342	
9 April	003 498	First: 156
13 July	003 602	Second: 104
8 October	003 734	Third: 132
5 January	003 932	Fourth: 198

6. £90

7. £166.40

8. £91.88

9. £128.42

10. £153.90

11. 189.9

12. 325.1

13. 257.0

14. 491.2

15. 115.584

16. 374.3

17. 285.2

18. 268.3

19. 255.4

20. 144.6

21. 179.1

22. £232

23. £139.44

24. £257.06

25. £174.33

26. £190.65

27. £126.19

28. £102.21

29. £250.50

30. £322.02

	Credit Tariff	Domestic Prepayment	Cheaper Tariff	Difference in tariffs
31.	£134.00	£136.00	Credit	£2.00
32.	£192.50	£184.50	Domestic	£8.00
33.	£247.40	£233.20	Domestic	£14.20
34.	£246.83	£248.42	Credit	£1.59
35.	£138	£147	Credit	£9.00
36.	£165.50	£162	Domestic	£3.50
37.	£210.50	£203.50	Domestic	£7.00
38.	£248.92	£206.66	Domestic	£42.26

EXERCISE 10c

1. £75.30

2. £87.87

3. £141.16

4. £131.75

5. £200.75

6. 5 p

7. 48 p

8. 55 p

9. 49 p

10. 37.5 p

11. 51.2 p	**14.** 56 p	**17.** 8; 16 minutes
12. 58 p	**15.** £1.48	**18.** £2.56
13. 20 p	**16.** £1.32	**19.** 18p; 12p

EXERCISE 10d

1. 51 p	**7.** £1.38	**13.** £9.71
2. £1.08	**8.** 96 p	**14.** £8.67
3. £2.65	**9.** £4.24	**15.** £1.02
4. £1.84	**10.** £2.54	**16.** £5.08
5. £8.70	**11.** £6.90	**17.** £1050
6. £1.04	**12.** £12.25	**18.** £30.72, £1597.44

EXERCISE 10e Ask pupils to check unit prices in their local supermarket. They will probably provide some surprising results! It does not always pay to buy large quantities, nor is it always easy to check unit prices. This is particularly true in greengrocery departments where prepacked goods are sold and priced in kilograms and loose goods sold and priced in pounds.

1. £1 per kg, £0.98 per kg; £2.94 for 3 kg
2. 1.74 p per oz, 2.8 p per oz; 27 p for $15\frac{1}{2}$ oz
3. 54 p per lge loaf, 61.7 p per lge loaf; 54 p for a large loaf
4. 3.3 p per envelope, 3.2 p per envelope; 32 p for ten
5. 5 p each, 4.2 p each; 50 p per dozen
6. 20 p each, 18 p each; £4.50 per box of 25
7. £3.20 per lb, £3.63 per lb; £8 for $2\frac{1}{2}$ lb
8. 16 p per kg, 13 p per kg, £6.50 for 50 kg
9. £1.70 per litre, £1.75 per litre; £8.50 for 5 litres
10. 21.5 p per square metre, 21.4 p per square metre; £3 for 14 m²
11. £1.17 per litre, £1.16 per litre; £5.80 for 5 litres
12. 4.5 p each, 4.4 p each; £1.05 for 24

EXERCISE 10f   **1.**

Date	Meter Reading	Number of units used in the specified quarter
3 January	20 436	
5 April	21 175	First: 739
2 July	21 650	Second: 475
8 October	22 173	Third: 523
5 January	22 859	Fourth: 686

2. Table from original questions with the following numbers.
16 291   15 843   448

448 at 8.2 p   36.74
                                               12.60
                                               49.34

3. Same layout as question with the following numbers.

4261   4118   143   148

                                               14.26
                                               66.60
                                               80.86

Average cost per week is £6.20 to nearst 10 p.

4. Same layout as question with the following numbers.
                                    £
                        21.50   21.50

                1107   71.07
                        92.57
                        13.58
                       106.45

5. 206

CHAPTER 11 Transformations and Congruency

EXERCISE 11a 1.

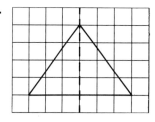

3.

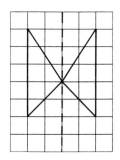

2.

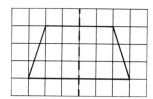

4.

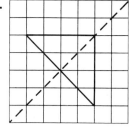

5.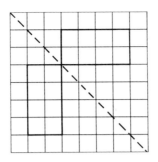

6.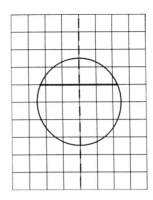

7.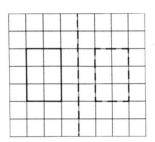

10.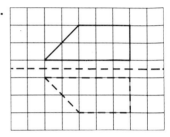

8.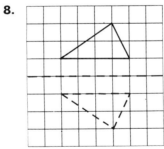

11.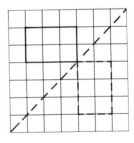

9.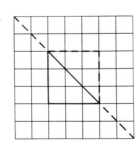

12.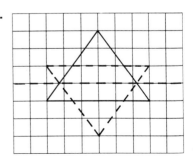

13.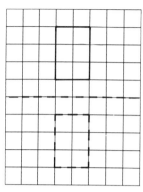

16.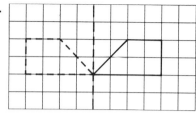

14.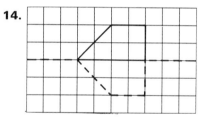

17.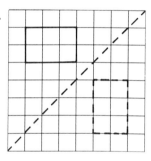

15.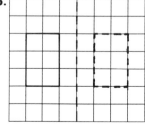

18.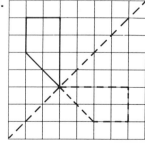

EXERCISE 11b 1.

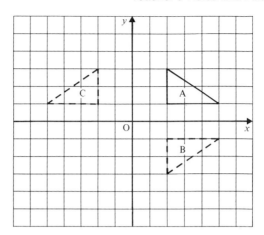

2.

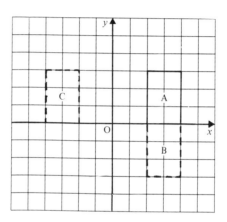

3.

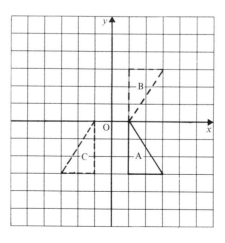

4.

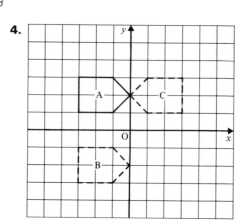

5.

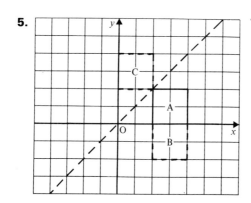

7.

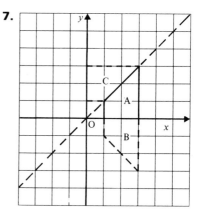

6.

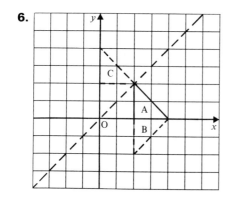

8.

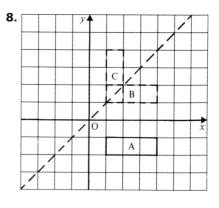

9. *x*-axis
10. *y*-axis
11. *x*-axis
12. *y* = *x*

13.

14.

15.

16.

17.
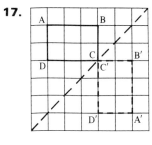

18.
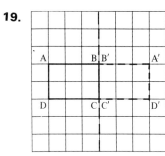

19.

20.
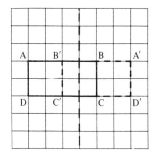

EXERCISE 11c   **1.** 90° anticlockwise   **3.** 180°   **5.** 90° clockwise
                    2. 90° clockwise   **4.** 180°   **6.** 90° clockwise

7.

11.

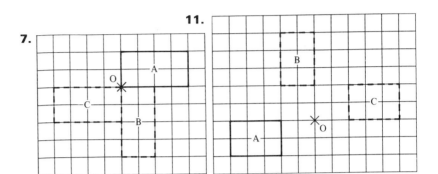

8.

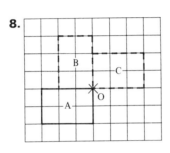

12.

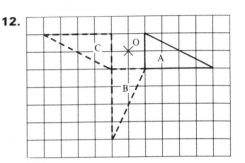

9.

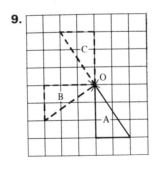

13.

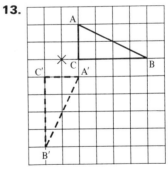

10.

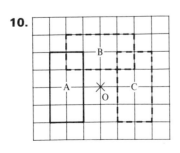

14.

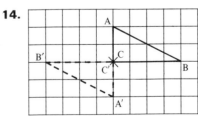

15.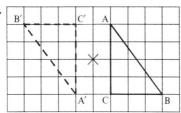

17.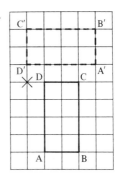

16.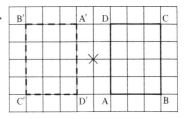

18.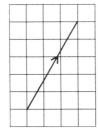

EXERCISE 11d   **1.** $\begin{pmatrix} 4 \\ 1 \end{pmatrix}$ **5.** $\begin{pmatrix} 3 \\ -2 \end{pmatrix}$ **9.** $\begin{pmatrix} 5 \\ 0 \end{pmatrix}$

2. $\begin{pmatrix} 2 \\ 3 \end{pmatrix}$ **6.** $\begin{pmatrix} 2 \\ -2 \end{pmatrix}$ **10.** $\begin{pmatrix} 0 \\ 2 \end{pmatrix}$

3. $\begin{pmatrix} 3 \\ 2 \end{pmatrix}$ **7.** $\begin{pmatrix} -3 \\ -2 \end{pmatrix}$ **11.** $\begin{pmatrix} -3 \\ 2 \end{pmatrix}$

4. $\begin{pmatrix} 1 \\ 3 \end{pmatrix}$ **8.** $\begin{pmatrix} -2 \\ -3 \end{pmatrix}$ **12.** $\begin{pmatrix} -4 \\ -1 \end{pmatrix}$

13.

15.

14.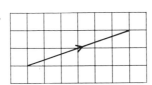

16.

17.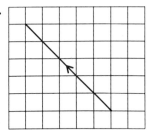

19.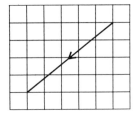

18.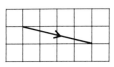

20.

21. $\begin{pmatrix} 4 \\ 1 \end{pmatrix}$

24. $\begin{pmatrix} 2 \\ -2 \end{pmatrix}$

22. $\begin{pmatrix} -5 \\ 0 \end{pmatrix}$

25. $\begin{pmatrix} -2 \\ -2 \end{pmatrix}$

23. $\begin{pmatrix} 4 \\ 3 \end{pmatrix}$

26. $\begin{pmatrix} 0 \\ 4 \end{pmatrix}$

27.–32.

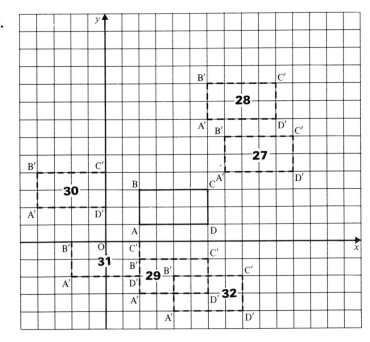

EXERCISE 11e There is sometimes more than one transformation possible—accept any possible answer.

Questions which are double underlined can be used for discussion. Question 19 in particular can be developed further: e.g. can you see two congruent parallelograms—why are they congruent? Another good discussion problem is to start with a parallelogram, draw in the diagonals and ask pupils to find two pairs of congruent triangles (don't ask them to justify answers) and then ask them what implications it has for the diagonals.

1. yes: a translation or rotation or reflection
2. no
3. yes: reflection
4. yes: translation or rotation or reflection
5. yes: rotation *NO*
6. no
7. yes: rotation
8. yes: reflection or rotation
9. yes: reflection
10. no
11.

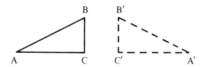

12. a)

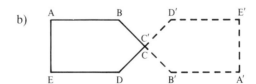

b)

13. a)

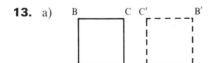

c)

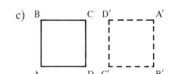

b)

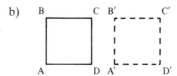

14. a) either a reflection; (5, −5) or a rotation; (2, −5)
   b) translation; (−1, 5)
   c) rotation; (−5, −3)
   d) translation
15. a) reflection in *y*-axis
   b) isosceles
   c) AB = 8 units, OC = 5 units
   d) 20 square units
16. reflection in the line AE, $A\hat{D}B = 90°$
17. a) rotation of 180° about C
   b) 38°
   c) alternate
   d) AB and DE are parallel.
18. a) DC = 10 cm
   b) E
   c) 4 cm
   d) parallelogram
19. a) 30°   b) 90°   c)90°
   d) ABDE is a trapezium.
20. a) reflection in DB
   b) reflection in AC
   c) rotation of 180° about E
   d) AB, BC, CD
   e) ABCD is a rhombus.

CHAPTER 12 Trigonometry

We strongly advise the use of scientific calculators, but all the exercises in this chapter can be done using trigonometric tables for sine, cosine and tangent and a simple calculator with square roots.

EXERCISE 12a
1. 6.32 cm	**4.** 5.28 cm	**7.** 7.55 cm	**10.** 15.5 cm
2. 52.2 cm	**5.** 3.58 cm	**8.** 9.54 cm	**11.** 16 cm
3. 16.1 cm	**6.** 19.4 cm	**9.** 27.4 cm	**12.** 3.57 cm

13. 9.43 cm	**23.** 15.4 m	**32.**
14. 10.9 cm	**24.** 26.7 cm	
15. 13.2 cm	**25.** 1.73 cm	
16. 30 cm	**26.** 0.917 cm	
17. 6 cm	**27.** 2.97 cm	
18. 90 cm	**28.** 21.2 cm	
19. 60 cm	**29.** 7.5 cm	
20. 16.6 cm	**30.** a) 2.83 cm	
21. 5 cm	b) 3.46 cm	
22. 8.87 cm	**31.** diagonal should be 2.56 m	

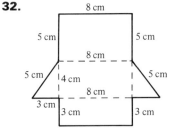

EXERCISE 12b

1. 0.2867	**3.** 1.248	**5.** 3.354
2. 6.314	**4.** 0.9195	**6.** 0.4705

7. 41.5°	**9.** 2.7°	**11.** 8.3°
8. 60.7°	**10.** 69.7°	**12.** 45.1°

13. 0.3090	**15.** 0.6845	**17.** 0.6129
14. 0.9455	**16.** 0.7815	**18.** 0.9882

19. 0.9631	**21.** 0.7771	**23.** 0.3040
20. 0.8829	**22.** 0.7205	**24.** 0.9659

25. 38.4°	**28.** 2.4°	**31.** 29.1°
26. 71.7°	**29.** 70.5°	**32.** 2.4°
27. 82.4°	**30.** 19.5°	**33.** 47.2°

34. 0.2679	**36.** 0.5358	**38.** 0.6444
35. 0.5358	**37.** 0.2419	**39.** 0.2419

EXERCISE 12c

1. tan, 20.6°	**3.** tan, 50.2°	**5.** cos, 42.8°
2. cos, 33.6°	**4.** sin, 53.1°	**6.** sin, 33.1°

7. 2.12 cm	**9.** 5.44 cm	**11.** 2.77 cm
8. 10.2 cm	**10.** 7.63 cm	**12.** 5.13 cm

13. 29.7°
14. a) 5.71 cm   b) 45.7 cm²
15. 4.82 m, 1.18 m
16. 9.97 cm
17. a) 26.0 m   b) 30°
c) RS = 69.3 m, RÔS = 60°, QP̂S = 72°, PS = 84.1 m
d) 219 m   e) 2430 m²

EXERCISE 12d For practical work a *clinometer* can be made which will measure angles of elevation and depression. Use a semicircle of card and mark it as shown. Attach a small weight on a flexible thread to act as a plumb line.

Note however that even with expert use this instrument is not accurate.

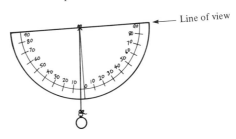

Line of view

1. DB̂C

3. a) BD̂C   b) EÂD

2. PQ̂R

4. a) QP̂S   b) QR̂S

5. b) 16.1 m   c) 17.7 m

6. 8.90 m

7. b) $x = 26.6°$, $y = 21.8°$

8. a) CÂB = 25°, AĈD = 15°, DĈB = 50° AD̂C = 140°

b) BD = 35.8, BA = 64.3 m   c) D is 28.6 m from A

EXERCISE 12e **1.** a) WẐY   b) ZŶX

2. a) UT̂P   b) ST̂R

c) TP̂Q = 19°, PT̂Q = 71°

3. a) ED̂B   b) ED̂C

c) AD̂B = 52°, AB̂D = 38°

4. a) 65°   b) 429 m

5. 60.2 m

6. Ĉ = 26.6°; 26.6°

7. 32.2 m   **10.** 48.8 m

8. 160 m   **11.** 202 m, 236 m, 34 m

9. 33.3 m   **12.** 119 m, 397 m

EXERCISE 12f **1.** a) 4.47 cm   b) 1.88 cm   c) 4.94 cm

2. a) 9.75 km   b) 3.5 km   c) 6.06 km   d) 35.7°

3. a) 17.5 cm   b) 31.0°   c) 118.0°   d) 135 cm²

4. a) 9.81 m   b) 9.87 m

5. a) BC = 4.66 m; Height of C = 5.66 m

b) BD = 9.00 m; 4.34 m

6. a) PS = 4.10 cm   b) QS = 2.87 cm   c) PQ̂S = 55°

d) QŜR = 35°   e) 2.01 cm   f) 6.10 cm

7. AC = 13.4 cm, AD = 14.6 cm

8. AB = 9.06 cm, BC = 4.66 cm, BD̂C = 25°

EXERCISE 12g **1.** 11.7 cm   **4.** 13.5 cm   **7.** 14.2 cm

2. 12.7 cm   **5.** 8.90 cm   **8.** a) 7.08 m   b) 3.75 m

3. 7.51 cm   **6.** 10.2 cm   **9.** a) 7 m   b) 35°   c) 8.55 cm

EXERCISE 12h **1.** A   **2.** A   **3.** C   **4.** B

EXERCISE 12i **1.** C   **2.** B   **3.** D   **4.** A

CHAPTER 13 Ratio and Proportion

EXERCISE 13a

1. $10\,\text{km} : 4\,\text{km} = 5 : 2$ **3.** $6\,\text{cm} : 15\,\text{cm} = 2 : 5$
2. $27\,\text{p} : £1 = 27 : 100$ **4.** $240 : 180 = 4 : 3$

5. $3 : 2$ **8.** $5 : 8$ **11.** $4 : 3$
6. $4 : 5$ **9.** $8 : 5$ **12.** $5 : 2$
7. $25 : 12$ **10.** $4 : 3$ **13.** $9 : 7$

14. $3 : 5 : 6$ **15.** $4 : 6 : 9$ **16.** $2 : 3 : 4$

17. $5 : 4$ **20.** $2 : 1$ **23.** $2 : 1$
18. $25 : 17$ **21.** $4 : 5$ **24.** $40 : 9$
19. $10 : 9$ **22.** $10 : 1$ **25.** $4 : 1$

26. $10 : 9$ **28.** $7 : 3$ **30.** $2 : 5$
27. $4 : 1$ **29.** $4 : 5$ **31.** $10 : 9$

32. $1 : 1.6$ **34.** $1 : 1.125$ **36.** $1 : 1.75$
33. $1 : 1.5$ **35.** $1 : 0.7$ **37.** $1 : 1.8$

38. $1 : 1\frac{1}{6}$ **40.** $1 : 3\frac{1}{3}$ **42.** $9 : 1\frac{4}{9}$
39. $1 : 1\frac{4}{7}$ **41.** $1 : \frac{3}{11}$ **43.** $1 : 1\frac{1}{4}$

44. $2\frac{2}{5}$ **46.** $3\frac{3}{4}$ **48.** $2\frac{2}{3}$
45. $1\frac{5}{7}$ **47.** $7\frac{1}{2}$ **49.** 28

EXERCISE 13b   **1.** $5 : 6$ **3.** $4 : 5$ **5.** $5 : 6$
2. $128 : 121$ **4.** $3 : 4$ **6.** $8 : 35$

EXERCISE 13c   **1.** $30\,\text{cm}, 50\,\text{cm}$ **6.** £16, £12, £8
2. $3\,\text{p}, 21\,\text{p}$ **7.** $63\,\text{p}, 18\,\text{p}, 9\,\text{p}$
3. $32\,\text{p}, 16\,\text{p}$ **8.** $16\,\text{cm}, 4\,\text{cm}, 12\,\text{cm}$
4. $8\,\text{mm}, 10\,\text{mm}$
5. £10, £15

9. Oxfam £63, RSPCA £105   **14.** 200
10. advertising 15 min,   **15.** a) $2 : 1$ b) $300\,\text{g}$
     programmes 90 min   **16.** Mr Brown 80 litres,
11. heating £56, lighting £16   Mrs Brown 60 litres
12. £1240   **17.** a) £2600 and £3400
13. Bill £15, Joanna £10   b) £2700 and £3300

EXERCISE 13d   **1.** a) $9\,\text{p}$ b) $27\,\text{p}$ **3.** a) $16\,\text{g}$ b) $144\,\text{g}$
2. a) 8 b) 40 **4.** $4\,\text{m}$ b) $20\,\text{m}$

5. 21
6. a) 15 m   b) 12 parcels
7. a) £40.50   b) 6 hours
8. 5.6 cm

9. 77 min
10. a) £2.25   b) 14 days
11. a) £126   b) 16 m²

EXERCISE 13e
1. a) 112 desks   b) 16 rows
2. a) 1800 helpings   b) 10 days
3. a) £252   b) 72

4. 24 rows
5. 3 h 36 min or 3.6 h
6. 4
7. 18

EXERCISE 13f
1. a) 8 months
    b) 10 cm
2. 84
3. 3
4. £140

5. 35 m
6. 16
7. 25 oz
8. 84 min
9. 5.2 m

10. a) 324 cm²
    b) 9
11. a) 25.6 mm
    b) 625 pages

EXERCISE 13g Exercises 13g and 13h can be used as preparation for dealing with maps and scale drawing in Chapter 14.

1. a) 80 cm   b) 32 cm   c) 420 cm
2. a) 30 km   b) 55 km   c) 36 km
3. a) 600 m   b) 2 km

4. 45 km
5. 264 km
6. 600 miles

7. a) 5 cm   b) 4½ cm   c) 16 cm
8. a) 2 cm   b) 12 cm   c) 2.4 cm
9. a) 6 cm   b) 20 cm   c) 5.6 cm
10. a) 54 cm   b) 23 cm
11. a) 7 cm   b) 5.75 cm

EXERCISE 13h
1. a) 100 m   b) 400 m
2. a) 5 km   b) 25 km
3. 72 m
4. 53 km
5. 15.5 km
6. 10 km

7. 1 : 40 000
8. 1 : 500 000
9. 1 : 200 000
10. 1 : 600
11. 1 : 10 000

12. 80 m
13. 20 km
14. 150 km
15. 5.75 km
16. 1.2 km

17. 8 cm
18. 60 cm
19. 3 cm
20. 5.5 cm
21. 9.3 cm

22. a) 5 cm, 3.2 cm   b) 100 km   c) 64 km
23. a) 88 km   b) 92 km
24. a) 4 km   b) 2.5 km   c) 9 cm
25. a) 160 m   b) 110 m   c) 4.5 cm
26. a) 10 km   b) 100 km²   c) 1 cm²   d) 600 km²
27. 2500 m²

EXERCISE 13i	**1.** $3 : 2$	**4.** $1 : 3.25$	**7.** $2.5\,\text{cm}$
	2. $12\,\text{m}, 27\,\text{m}$	**5.** 4 days	**8.** 451
	3. $25 : 13$	**6.** $87.5\,\text{km}$	

EXERCISE 13j	**1.** £15, £57	**4.** $4 : 3$	**7.** $1.4\,\text{kg}$
	2. $64 : 27$	**5.** $12\,\text{cm}$	**8.** $3200\,\text{cm}^2$
	3. $6\frac{2}{3}$	**6.** $312\,\text{m}$	

EXERCISE 13k **1.** C   **2.** D   **3.** A   **4.** B   **5.** D

CHAPTER 14 Scale Drawing

For most purposes the emphasis should be on *accurate* drawing using any appropriate instruments *and checks*: for example if a protractor is used to draw a right angle it can be checked with a set square or even by eye.

EXERCISE 14a
1. a) AB = 6.2 cm, AD = 4.3 cm
   b) AC = BD = 7.5 cm, yes
2. a) PR = 4.8 cm, PQ = RQ = 8.0 cm
   b) isosceles   d) $\hat{P} = \hat{R} = 72\frac{1}{2}°$, $\hat{Q} = 35°$; $180°$
3. a) $\hat{W}$ and $\hat{X}$ are obtuse, $\hat{Y}$ and $\hat{Z}$ are acute
   b) $\hat{W} = 110°$, $\hat{X} = 151°$, $\hat{Y} = 38°$, $\hat{Z} = 61°$
   c) WX = 4.1 cm, XY = 4.8 cm, YZ = 11 cm, ZW = 4.2 cm,
      WY = 8.7 cm, ZX = 6.9 cm

EXERCISE 14b The questions give straight line distances to measure so that there is no need to mark the pages but for more practical work duplicated maps could be used. Routes round road systems or coastlines for example, could then be measured either by marking the maps and measuring sections of the route or by 'walking' compasses or dividers along the route. Question 9 can be used to *estimate* distances, e.g. estimate the distance from Long Buckley to East Haddon by road. (It is about 4 km, accept $3\frac{1}{2}$ to $4\frac{1}{2}$ km).

1. AB = 80 cm, BC = 72 cm
2. PQ = 30.4 cm, PS = 20.4 cm
3. YZ = 42.5 km, ZX = 60 km
4. DE = 128 m, DF = 184 m
5. a) AB = 7.8 cm, BC = 6.4 cm, CA = 10.1 cm
   b) AB = 78 cm, BC = 64 cm, CA = 101 cm
6. a) PQ = 50 m   b) RQ = 39 m
7. a) 180 km   c) 310 km
   b) 195 km   d) 150 km
8. a) 308 km   c) 56 km
   b) 200 km   d) 156 km
9. a) 4 km   b) 5.6 km   c) 3.0 km
10. width of room = 3.7 m   width of unit and fridge = 3.6 m; yes

EXERCISE 14c

1. $\hat{A} = 53°$, $\hat{B} = 62°$, $\hat{C} = 65°$
2. $\hat{P} = 73\frac{1}{2}°$, $\hat{Q} = 52\frac{1}{2}°$, $R = 54°$
3. $\hat{L} = 54\frac{1}{2}°$, $\hat{M} = 28°$, $\hat{N} = 97\frac{1}{2}°$
4. $\hat{L} = \hat{M} = 62°$, $\hat{N} = 56°$
5. $\hat{Y} = \hat{Z} = 71°$, $\hat{X} = 39°$
6. $\hat{P} = 91°$, $\hat{Q} = 38\frac{1}{2}°$, $\hat{R} = 50\frac{1}{2}°$
7. $\hat{C} = 63°$, BC $= 8.1$ cm, AC $= 8.7$ cm
8. $\hat{N} = 36°$, LN $=$ NM $= 9.7$ cm
9. BC $= 6.2$ cm, AC $= 7.7$ cm, $\hat{C} = 107°$
10. $\hat{R} = 55°$, PR $= 9.0$ cm, RQ $= 3.9$ cm.
11. $\hat{Z} = 60°$, XZ $=$ ZY $= 7.8$ cm
12. LN $= 7.6$ cm, MN $= 6.8$ cm, $\hat{N} = 83°$
13. BC $= 5.8$ cm, $\hat{C} = 119\frac{1}{2}°$, $\hat{B} = 35\frac{1}{2}°$
14. PQ $= 13.0$ cm, $\hat{P} = 47\frac{1}{2}°$, $\hat{Q} = 42\frac{1}{2}°$
15. LN $= 10$ cm, $\hat{L} = 45°$, $\hat{N} = 90°$
16. XZ $= 9.1$ cm, $\hat{X} = 69\frac{1}{2}°$, $\hat{Z} = 38\frac{1}{2}°$
17. DC $= 9.3$ cm, $\hat{C} = \hat{D} = 90°$
18. $\hat{B} = 53°$, $\hat{C} = 127°$, $\hat{D} = 90°$
19. $A\hat{B}C = 92\frac{1}{2}°$, $\hat{C} = 80\frac{1}{2}°$, $A\hat{D}C = 115°$ (BD $= 9.7$ cm)
    AD $= 6.3$ cm
20. CD $= 7.1$ cm, $\hat{C} = \hat{D} = 108°$
21. AB $=$ AC $= 7.4$ cm
22. 10 cm
23. 6.5 cm
24. 10.8 cm, 5.3 cm

EXERCISE 14d There is more practice on map scales in Exercises 13g and 13h.

1. AB $= 8$ cm, BC $= 5.5$ cm, AC $= 6.2$ cm
2. PQ $= 9$ cm, QR $= 4.5$ cm, RS $= 6$ cm, SP $= 4.6$ cm
3. AB $= 9$ cm, BC $= 7.2$ cm
4. AB $=$ GH $= 6$ cm, BC $=$ FG $= 2.25$ cm, CD $=$ EF $= 3.75$ cm,
   DE $= 5.5$ cm, HA $= 10$ cm
5. AB $= 8$ cm, BC $= 6.4$ cm
6. WX $= 10.2$ cm, WZ $= 7.5$ cm
7. AC $= 46$ cm, BC $= 55$ cm
8. SR $= 193$ m, SQ $= 201$ m
10. AB $= 8.1$ m
11. a) ii) CD $= \frac{1}{2}$ m   iii) trapezium

b) i) 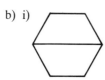   c) i)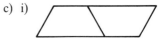

iii) 0.87 m, 1 m, 0.87 m   iii) 1.8 m

EXERCISE 14e **1.** AC = 18.9 m, DC = 12.0 m
  2. 41.6 km
  3. 2.8 m
  4. a) 7.4 m b) suitable scale 1 cm to $\frac{1}{2}$ m

EXERCISE 14f In questions 11 to 14 pupils should be asked to estimate the size of angles first, as a check on their measurements. This will probably need practice so give them a duplicated sheet of drawn angles to estimate. Another method to aid angle estimation is to ask them to draw angles of say 30°, 45°, 60° by eye and then measure them.

1. 072°   **5.** 115°   **9.** 065°
2. 108°   **6.** 290°   **10.** 075°
3. 012°   **7.** 244°
4. 122°   **8.** 229°

11. 105°   **12.** 068°   **13.** 072°   **14.** 115°
15. a) 038°   b) 134°   c) 218°

16.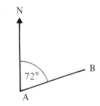

18.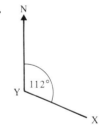

17.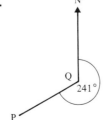

19.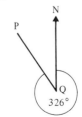

20.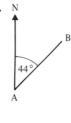

22.

24.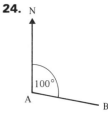

21.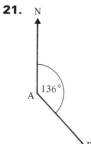

23.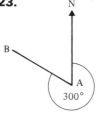

25.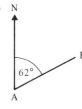

EXERCISE 14g **1.** a) N 80° E   b) 080°   **4.** a) S 62° W   b) 242°
 2. a) S 60° E   b) 120°   **5.** a) N 42° W   b) 318°
 3. a) S 70° E   b) 110°   **6.** a) S 85° W   b) 265°

7.

9. 124°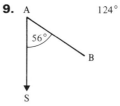

11. 301°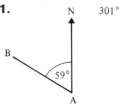

8. 333°

10. 052°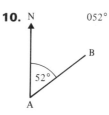

12. 098°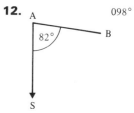

13. 1. N 72° E   5. S 65° E   9. N 65° E
        2. S 72° E   6. N 70° W   10. N 75° E
        3. N 12° E   7. S 64° W
        4. S 58° E   8. S 49° W

EXERCISE 14h **1.** a) $x = 130°$, $y = 50°$ b) 050°
                        d) BC = 15.6 m
                  2. a) $\hat{A} = 50°$, $\hat{B} = 50°$, $\hat{C} = 80°$
                        c) BA = 64 m, BC = 50 m
                        d) i) 080°   ii) 130°   iii) 260°
                  3. a) 7.8 km   b) 5.2 km
                        c) 070°   d) 12.8 km
                        e) 15.4 minutes
                  4. a) $\hat{A} = 78°$, $\hat{B} = 34°$, $\hat{C} = 68°$
                        c) CA = 8.3 km, CB = 8.7 km
                        d) $A\hat{C}D = 78°$
                        f) AD = 8.1 km
                        g) 088°
                        h) 282°

EXERCISE 14i **1.** a) 110 m   b) 47 m   **3.** $26\frac{1}{2}°$
                  2. 16 m   **4.** 22°

CHAPTER 15 Enlargements and Similarity

EXERCISE 15a

1.

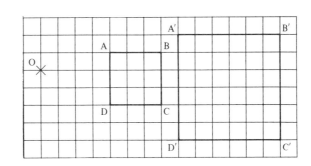

2.

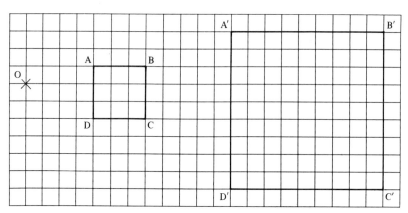

3. a)

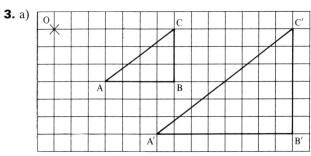

b)

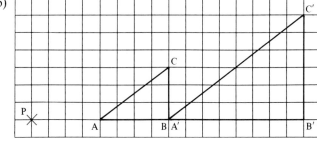

c)

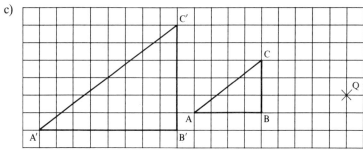

d)

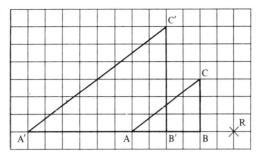

e)

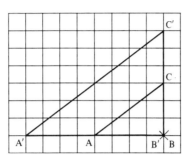

Changing the centre of enlargements changes the position of the image but not its size.

4.

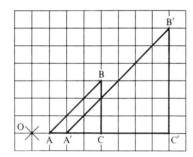

5.

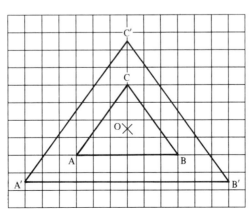

6.

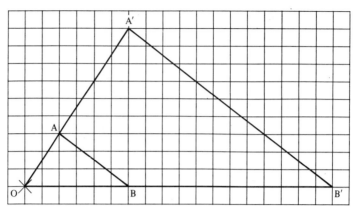

7.

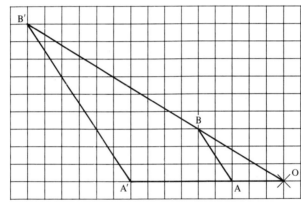

8.

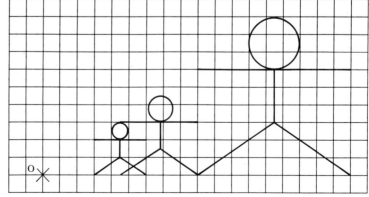

9.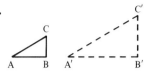

12.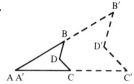

10.

13.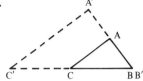

11.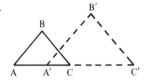

14.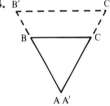

15. a) D   b) E   c) A
16. a) i) Q   ii) R   b) QR   c) MN
17. a) Y X̂ Z   b) XT   c) Y
18. (0, 1), the centre of enlargement
19. A(1, 1)

EXERCISE 15b There is a simple instrument (sometimes called a pantograph), available from toy shops, for drawing enlargements. If one of these can be produced, and demonstrated, then how it works, and what scale factor it uses, can be investigated.

1. (0, 0), 3   **3.** (−2, 0), 2   **5.** (0, 0), 2
2. (5, 7), 2   **4.** (2, 0), $1\frac{1}{2}$ **6.** (10, 0), 3

EXERCISE 15c **1.** a) 6 cm   b) 12 cm   c) 4 cm
2. a) 60 cm   b) 250 cm (2.5 m)   c) 45°   d) 6
3. a) 9 cm   b) 6 cm   c) 1 cm   d) 60°, 30°
4. a) 8 cm   b) 2   c) 3.5 cm
5. a) (i) 10 cm   (ii) 6 cm   b) (i) 15 cm^2 (ii) 60 cm^2 c) 4
6. a) (i) 20 cm   (ii) 6 cm   b) 48 cm^2, 300 cm^2 c) 6.25

7. a) 45° b) △ABC is isosceles and right angled. AB = 10 cm
   c) 10 m, 45°
8. a) 5 b) 5.6 cm, 2.1 cm c) 112 cm, 42 cm d) 5 cm, 102 cm
9. a) 4 cm b) 6 cm c) 8 cm³, 216 cm³ d) 12 cm
10. a) 2.4 km   b) 2 km   c) 50°

EXERCISE 15d **1.** 2   **4.** 4   **7.** 10 cm
                  2. 3   **5.** 2   **8.** 6 cm
                  3. 1.5   **6.** 2   **9.** 8 cm

10. a) AD   b) and c)
     d) 2.5 cm

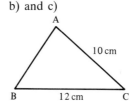

11. a) AÊD   b) and c)
     d) AB = 8 cm
        AD = 5 cm

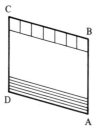

12. a) 3 cm by 2 cm
     b) The light from the top edge of the object goes *down* through the lens
        forming the lower edge of the image. Similarly the lower edge of the
        object reflects light up through the lens forming the top edge of the
        image.
     c)

CHAPTER 16 Circles and Symmetry

In this chapter much emphasis is placed on symmetry. A general discussion of its
implications would be appropriate here.

EXERCISE 16a **1.** ADE   **4.** AB, BC, CD and AD
                  2. ABC   **5.** AF, CD and FBD
                  3. PA and PD   **6.** CD, BC and AB

7.

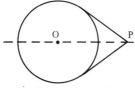

they are equal

8.

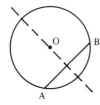

a) 90°
b) at the midpoint

9.

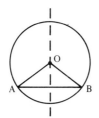

a) isosceles
b) congruent triangles

10.

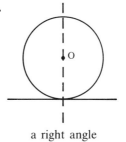

a right angle

11.

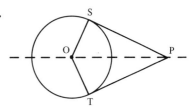

congruent triangles

EXERCISE 16b Some questions require the use of trigonometry.

1.

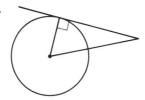

2.

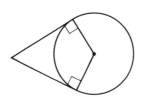

3.

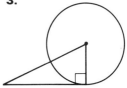

4.

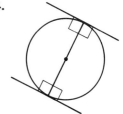

5. 10 cm
6. 1.5 cm
7. 60°
8. 53.1°

9. 12 cm
10. 11.7 cm
11. a) 5.66 cm   b) 45°
12. a) 6.63 cm   b) 56.4°

EXERCISE 16c Pythagoras' result and trigonometry are needed in this exercise.

1. a) 8 cm   b) 16 cm
2. 15 cm
3. 5 cm
4. a) 8.94 cm   b) 17.9 cm
5. 11.2 cm
6. a) 51.3°   b) 102.6°
7. a) 35.4°   b) 54.6°   c) 109.2°
8. 9.64 cm
9. a) 43.3°   b) 46.7°   c) 93.4°
10. a) 54.9°   b) 70.2°
11. a) 4.12 cm   b) 6.86 cm   c) 13.72 cm
12. a) 11.7 cm   b) 8.58 cm   c) 17.2 cm
13. a) 9.58 cm   b) 14.4 cm
14. a) 18.1 cm   b) 32.0 cm

EXERCISE 16d
1. a) 9.17 cm   b) 23.6°   c) 47.2°
2. a) 15 cm   b) 40 cm   c) 53.1°
3. a) 28°   b) 10.7 cm   c) 9.40 cm
4. a) 6.38 cm   b) 13.6 cm   c) 10.6 cm   d) 5.63 cm

EXERCISE 16e This exercise revises the 'angle in a semicircle' result.

1. $d = 90°, e = 36°$
2. $f = g = 90°$
3. $h = 90°, i = 52°$
4. $j = 90°, k = l = 45°$
5. $m = 90°, n = 54°$
6. $p = 90°, q = 30°, 2q = 60°$
7. $r = 90°, s = 69°$
8. $4x = 40°, y = 50°, 9x = 90°$
9. a) 3.06 cm   b) 6.74 cm
10. a) 10.2 cm   b) 9.55 cm
11. a) 9.24 cm   b) 4.62 cm
12. a) 45°   b) 90   c) 14.1 cm

EXERCISE 16f
1. $d = 20°, e = 20°, f = 140°$
2. $g = 62°, h = 62, i = 28°$
3. $j = 45°, k = 45°$
4. $l = 90°, m = 54°$
5. $p = 25°, q = 65°$
6. $d = 43°, e = 90°, f = 43°$
7. $h = 90°, i = 45°$
8. $j = 40°, k = 65°, l = 25°$
9. $p = 61°, q = 29°, r = 122°$
10. $m = 56°, n = 124°, p = 28°$
11. $x = 30°, 2x = 60°, 4x = 120°$
12. $s = 58°, t = 58°, u = 32°, v = 58°$

CHAPTER 17

Many of the exercises in this chapter can be used for oral work in class.

EXERCISE 17a
1. not possible
2. $8y$
3. $3x$
4. not possible
5. $4p$
6. $9x + 9$
7. $5x + 11y$
8. $3x + 2y$
9. $6a + b$
10. $5 - y$
11. not possible
12. $6t$
13. $4y - 2x$
14. $3a$
15. 0

EXERCISE 17b
1. $18b$
2. $3ab$
3. $15ab$
4. $-15a$
5. $-32p$
6. $-20r$
7. $-6a^2$
8. $2x^2$
9. $24xy$
10. $-6x$
11. $18p^2$
12. $-50y$
13. $-16y$
14. $-20r^2$
15. $10st$

EXERCISE 17c
1. $40x - 16$
2. $15 - 10x$
3. $8x^2 + 6x$
4. $10x + 35$
5. $15 - 12a$
6. $20x - 4x^2$
7. $12x - 9$
8. $12 - 42a$
9. $15x^2 - 10x$

10. $8x + 13$
11. $6x - 8$
12. $-x - 11$
13. $2x + 18$
14. $12x - 3$
15. $10x + 6$
16. $8x + 19$
17. $-3x - 9$
18. $21 - 3x$
19. $11x + 26$
20. $21x + 30$
21. $24x - 13$
22. $12x - 12$
23. $19x - 16$
24. $-13x - 14$

EXERCISE 17d
1. $3(x + 2)$
2. $4(a + 3)$
3. $5(5t - 1)$
4. $3(4x - 3)$
5. $4(3x + 2)$
6. $5(3 - 2x)$
7. $5(2x - 1)$
8. $3(2b + 3)$
9. $3(a - 3)$
10. $4(2 - 3x)$
11. $7(1 + 2t)$
12. $3(7x + 3)$

13. $5(x + 2y)$
14. $6(4x - 3y)$
15. $4(3x - y)$
16. $8(a + 3b)$
17. $5(2x - y)$
18. $3(a + 2b)$
19. $5(5s + t)$
20. $3(3x - 4y)$
21. $4(3x + 2y)$
22. $5(3a - 2b)$
23. $3(2a + 3b)$
24. $7(2x - 3y)$

25. $x(x + 5)$
26. $a(a - 3)$
27. $x(7 - x)$
28. $x(x - 9)$
29. $t(t + 10)$
30. $x(5 - x)$
31. $x(x + 8)$
32. $b(b - 9)$
33. $a(8 - a)$

34. $2x(2x + 1)$
35. $5a(2a - 3)$
36. $4x(3x + 2)$
37. $7x(1 - 2x)$
38. $3x(3x - 2)$
39. $2t(t + 2)$
40. $3y(3y - 5)$
41. $4p(1 + 3p)$
42. $5x(x + 2)$
43. $3a(3 - a)$
44. $4z(3z - 1)$
45. $5q(5 - 2q)$

EXERCISE 17e
1. C
2. A
3. D
4. D
5. C
6. B
7. B
8. D

EXERCISE 17f
1. a) $21x^2$ b) $-4y^2$
2. a) $49x + 14$ b) $-6x + 12$ c) $-10 + 15x$
3. a) $26x + 6$ b) $11x + 2$ c) $27x + 11$
4. a) $7(a - 2b)$ b) $x(x - 3)$
5. a) $4(2b - 3c)$ b) $2x(x - 3)$

EXERCISE 17g
1. a) $-32a^2$ b) $35x^2$
2. a) $-18 - 4x$ b) $21 - 12x$ c) $-5x^2 - 15x$
3. a) $23x + 17$ b) $18x + 4$ c) $-x - 3$
4. a) $5(y - 3x)$ b) $a(3 - 2a)$
5. a) $\dfrac{5 \mid 35}{6 \mid 48}$ b) $2n + n^2$ c) $n(2 + n)$

CHAPTER 18 Loci

EXERCISE 18a There is plenty of room for discussion in this exercise. Be fairly generous in terms of what's acceptable and what is not. Use teaching aids and models whenever possible. A globe is particularly useful. Additional examples will probably come easily to mind. OS maps may be used for questions similar to question 22.

1.   6.

2. _____

3.

7.

8. _____ Path of hubcap
_____ Road

4.

9.

Door

5.

10.

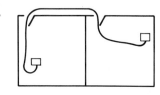

11.

18. a)

b)

12.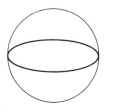

19.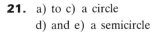

20. a) to e) a straight line

13.

21. a) to c) a circle
d) and e) a semicircle

14.

15. *one*

22.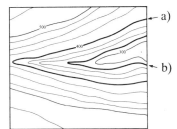

16. a)

b)

17.

23.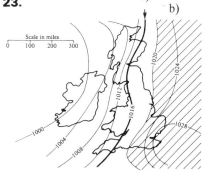

EXERCISE 18b **1.** a) The straight line drawn parallel to the bottom edge of the page and 5 cm from it.
   b) The straight line drawn parallel to the right hand edge of the page and 3 cm from it.

2. The two straight lines on the page that are parallel to AB and 5 cm from it (one above and one below).

3. a) a circle, centre C, radius 15 cm
   b) a circle, centre A, radius 15 cm
   c) a circle, centre C, radius 15 cm
   d) a circle, centre A, radius 30 cm
   a) and (c) are identical

4. a) the arc of a circle, radius 40 cm, whose centre lies on BC
   b) the arc of a circle, radius varying from 0 to 80 cm, whose centre is at the midpoint of BC
   c) part of the sphere, centre C, radius 80 cm

5. the perpendicular bisector of XY

6. the bisector of the angle PÔR

EXERCISE 18c **1.** a) a circle, centre A, radius 4 cm
   b) a circle, centre B, radius 4 cm
   c) the perpendicular bisector of AB; no

2. a) the perpendicular bisector of PR
   b) a circle, centre Q, radius 10 cm; yes

3. a) a circle, centre O, radius OM
   b) the diameter through M

4.

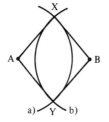

AXBY is a rhombus

5.

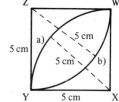

WXYZ is a square

6. The straight line drawn parallel to AB and 6 cm away from it; there is a second straight line on the opposite side of AB.

7.
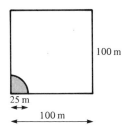

8.
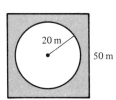

9.
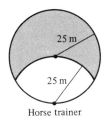

10.
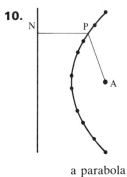

a parabola

11.
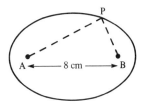

An ellipse or oval

12.
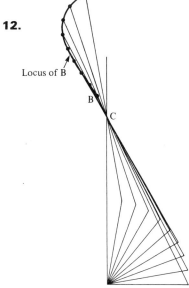

The maximum distance of B from the front of the cabinet is approximately 6.4 cm.

13.
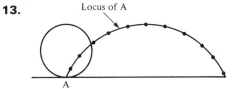

Locus of A

EXERCISE 18d **1.** a circle, centre A, radius 1.3 cm
2. a) a quarter of a circle, centre A, radius AD, i.e. 8 cm
b) a quarter of a circle, centre A, radius AC, i.e. 13.3 cm; no; C travels further than D

3.

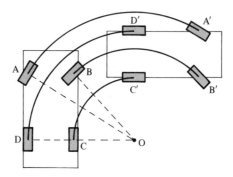

Each wheel moves through a quarter of a circle, centre 0, whose radius is the distance of the wheel from 0.

4. a) a circle, radius 2 cm, which is concentric with the large circle
b) a circle, radius 6 cm, which is concentric with the large circle

5.

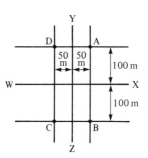

ABCD is a rectangle

6. the semicircle on AB as diameter; if C is marked on the opposite side of AB the locus is the other half of the same circle
7. the bisector of $\hat{ABC}$

8.

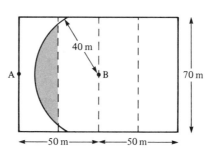

CHAPTER 19 Graphs

EXERCISE 19a Graphs from newspapers and other sources can be used for discussion.

1. a) i) \$1.25   ii) \$1
   b) It looks at first sight as though the value of £1 slumped to zero in April; because the scale of the vertical axis starts at \$1, the variation in the exchange rate appears greater than it is.
2. a) No; the horizontal axis has no scale and is not labelled.
   b) No, except that both motorcycles reached a speed of 60 m.p.h.
   c) Probably it is intended to show that whatever is represented by the black line is better than that represented by the broken line.
3. a) No
   b) The number of passengers fell and then recovered to the same level again.
   c) how the number of passengers varied compared to the numbers using the service at the beginning of 1980
4. a) that a person loses weight more rapidly using 'B plan'
   b) to emphasise the weight loss
   c) For many reasons, e.g. the 'ordinary diet' is not known—it may be bars of chocolate, two different people tend to lose weight at different rates even on identical diets. Starting the scale at 60 kg emphasises the actual weight loss.
5. a) that there are none left
   b) Probably 12 or 13 if the claim is still true after 4 applications
   c) The divisions are not of equal value.
   d) It is really impossible to say, but if the claim that it halves the number of grey hairs each time is true, then in theory it will never get rid of them all, although in practice it might after 9 or so applications.

EXERCISE 19b Graphs drawn to half scale

1.

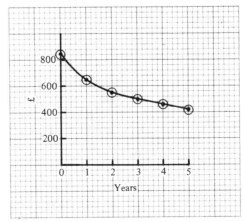

     a) £520   b) £200   c) £40

2.

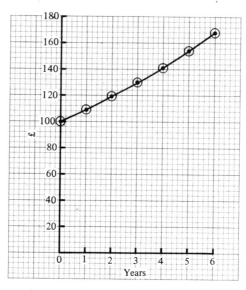

a) £135   b) 4.7 yrs   c) 9%

3.

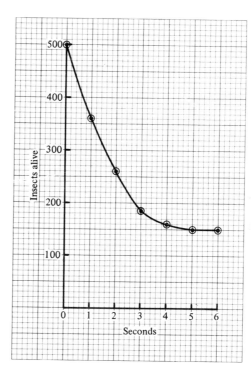

a) 170   b) 2.1 sec   c) Probably not, but can't tell

4.

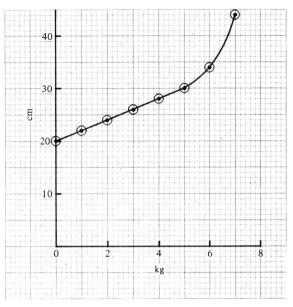

a) 20 cm   b) No   c) The spring gave way.

EXERCISE 19c Graphs drawn to half scale

1.

x	1	2	3	4	5
y	3	12	27	48	75

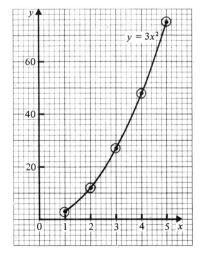

18.75, 1.6

2.

d	0	1	2	3	4	5	6
A	0	$\frac{1}{2}$	2	4.5	8	12.5	18

2.8; 19 hours (to the nearest hour)

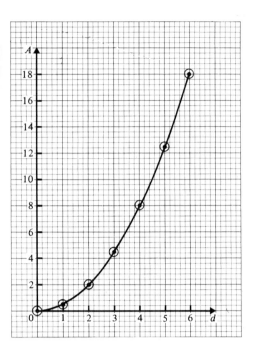

3.

t	-3	-2	-1	-0.5	0	0.5	1	2	3
s	45	20	5	1.25	0	1.25	5	20	45

a) 11.25, 31.25
b) -1.4 and 1.4

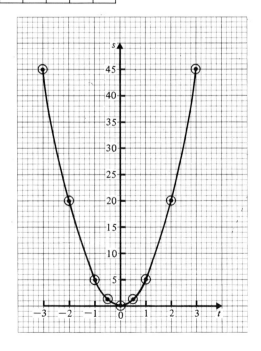

4. a)

b	20	30	40	50	60	70	80	90	100	110
l	180	120	90	72	60	51	45	40	36	33
p	400	300	260	244	240	242	250	260	272	286

b) $p = 2l + 2b$
e) 60, 60

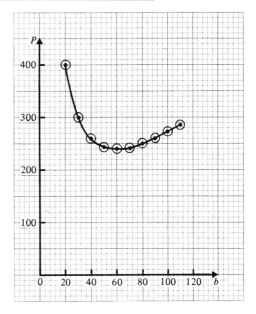

EXERCISE 19d Graphs drawn to half scale

1. a) $y = 2$ b) $x = 3$ c) $y = 1$ d) $y = -3$
2. a) 2   b) $-\frac{1}{2}$ c) $\frac{1}{2}$ d) 0

3.

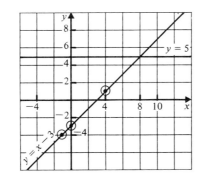

b)

x	−1	0	4
y	−4	−3	1

d) (8, 5)

4.

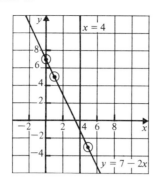

b)

x	0	1	5
y	7	5	-3

c) (4, −1)

5.

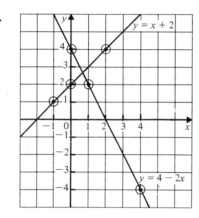

a)

x	0	1	4
y	4	2	-4

b)

x	-1	0	2
y	1	2	4

c) $x = 0.7$,
   $y = 2.7$ (on graph paper)
   $x = 0.5$,
   $y = 2.5$ (on 5 mm squares)

6. a) i) 1   ii) (0, 0)   iii) $y = x$
   b) i) 1   ii) (0, −2)   iii) $y = x - 2$

7. a) i) −1   ii) (0, 0)   iii) $y = -x$
   b) i) −1   ii) (0, 3)   iii) $y = -x + 3$

8.

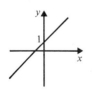

a)

b)

c)

d)

EXERCISE 19e Graphs drawn to half scale

1.

x	y
-3	9
-2	4
-1	1
-0.5	0.25
0	0
0.5	0.25
1	1
2	4
3	9

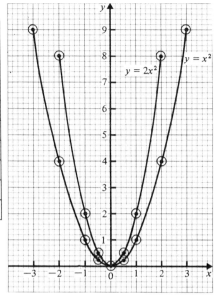

3.

x	y
-2	8
-1	2
-0.5	0.5
0	0
0.5	0.2
1	2
2	8

2.

x	y
-3	-9
-2	-4
-1	-1
-0.5	-0.25
0	0
0.5	-0.25
1	-1
2	-4
3	-9

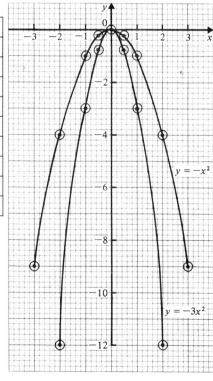

4.

x	y
-2	-12
-1	-3
-0.5	-0.75
0	0
0.5	-0.75
1	-3
2	-12

EXERCISE 19f Graphs drawn to half scale

1.

x	y
−4	8
−3	4.5
−2	2
−1	0.5
0	0
1	0.5
2	2
3	4.5
4	8

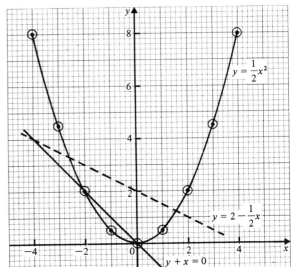

2.

x	y
−3	−13.5
−2	−6
−1	−1.5
−0.5	−0.38
0	0
0.5	−0.38
1	−1.5
2	−6
3	−13.5

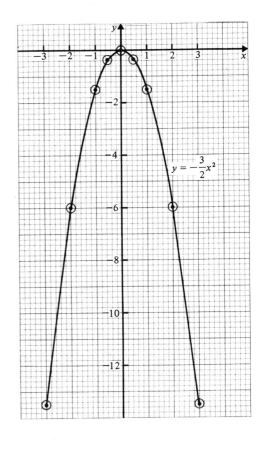

3.

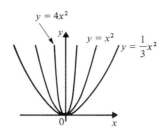

4. a) 1.1   b) 2.5

5. a) 2.25   b) −2 and 2   c) 1.4

6.

x	−4	−3	1
y	4	3	−1

(0, 0), (−2, 2)

7.

x	−2	0	2
y	3	2	1

a) (−2.6, 3.3), (1.6, 1.2)
b) (−4, 4)
c) $y + x = 0$ and $y = 2 - \frac{1}{2}x$

8. a)   c) $y = -x^2$

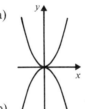

b)

9. a)

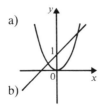

b)

c) Correct values are (1.6, 2.6), (−0.6, 0.4); accept answers within reasonable range of these values.

EXERCISE 19g Graphs drawn to half scale.

Much of this exercise can and should be used for discussion. It is important that the impossibility of division by zero is brought out, and the fact that a/x has no meaning when $x = 0$ means that there is no point on the graph.

1.

x	0.1	0.2	0.4	0.5	1	2	4	5
y	10	5	2.5	2	1	0.5	0.25	0.2

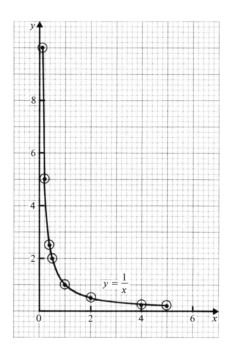

2. a) Values of y decrease.
b) Values of y increase.
c) 100, 1000
d) No

3.

x	-5	-4	-2	-1	-0.5	-0.4	-0.2	-0.1
y	-0.2	-0.25	-0.5	-1	-2	-2.5	-5	-10

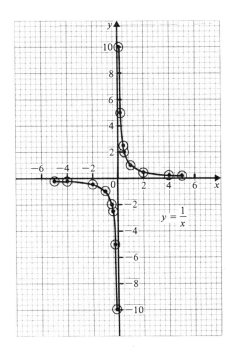

c) No

4.

x	−5	−2	−1	−0.5	−0.4	−0.25	0.25	0.4	0.5	1	2	5
y	−0.4	−1	−2	−4	−5	−8	8	5	4	2	1	0.4

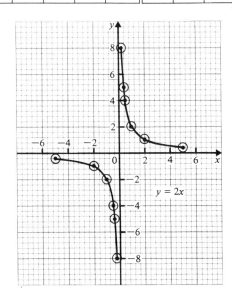

EXERCISE 19h

1.

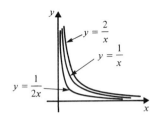

2.

x	10	20	40	50
y	10	5	2.5	2

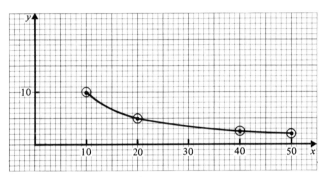

Graph drawn to half scale

a) 6.7 s (accept 6.5 – 6.8)
b) 2.2 s (accept 2.2 – 2.5)
c) 5.5 m/s

3. a) i) 300   ii) 180   iii) 90

b) $CN = 900$ or $C = \dfrac{900}{N}$ or $N = \dfrac{900}{C}$

c)

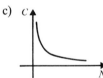   or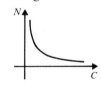

4. a) 0.8 m/s   b) 0.4 m/s   c) 20

d) speed $= \dfrac{20}{\text{width}}$

e) It is very unlikely; several factors affect the flow of water in a river apart from width.

EXERCISE 19i 1. B   2. C   3. A   4. C   5. C   6. C   7. B   8. A

CHAPTER 20 Revision Exercises

These exercises are a mixed selection of problems, a few of which involve work from earlier books.

EXERCISE 20a
1. a) 100   b) 144
2. a) 820 m   b) 30 inches   c) 1.05 pm or 13.05
3. 7 lb
4. a) $1 + 7x$ b) $3(x + 3)$
5. 750 cm^3
6. $p = 90°$, $q = 55°$
7. 40%
8. £28 000

9.

	Rental	£19.45
11.12.85 meter reading 027 658		
14.3.86 meter reading 030 856		
Units used 3198		
Units at 5p per unit		£159.90
Total (exclusive of VAT)		£179.35
VAT at 15%		£26.90
Total payable		£206.25

10. a) -10 b) $u = s + at$
11. a) $\frac{3}{4}$ b) -3 c) $\frac{1}{6}$

12.

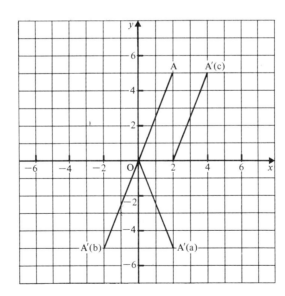

a) $(2, -5)$ b) $(-2, -5)$ c) $(4, 5)$

13. a) 51.9°   b) 0.5878   c) 8.8°
14. 266 cm (accept 255 – 270 cm)
15. £105.60

EXERCISE 20b **1.** a) $1\frac{1}{12}$ b) 0.04
2. The 2 gallon mark
3. 69 m.p.h (68.75 m.p.h should be rejected as an unreasonable attempt at accuracy given the approximate conversion).
4. a) 4   b) $x(x - 7)$

5.

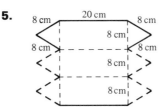

and other possible configurations

6. a) 30 cm, 75 cm² b) 31.4 cm, 78.5 cm²
7. a) 7 a.m.   b) 8 pm   c) 8 hours
8. a) BD   b) $w = 42°$, $x = 110°$, $y = 20°$
9. a) $\frac{2}{5}$ b) 0.4
10. £225
11. $C = 20 + 12n$
12. a) 25 cm   b) 36.9°
13. a)

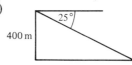

b) 858 m to 3 s.f.
14. a) $1\frac{1}{2}$ hours   b) 1 hour   c) 45 miles   d) 45 m.p.h.
15. a) About 13 miles   b) 16 miles
c) A63/A61 or A19/M62 (A1041/A645 is possible but is much longer)
d) 4   e) 1 : 350 000
f) 10.5 miles

EXERCISE 20c In question 15 explain the significance of the heavy and light type : heavy type denotes through trains, light type denotes connecting services.

1. a) 25%   b) $\frac{1}{4}$
2. a) 6   b) £30
3. a) £41   b) 286 Ff
4. a) $a = c - b$ b) $r = \dfrac{C}{2\pi}$

5. a) 9   b)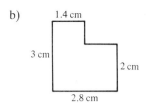

6. a) 6   b) 7
7. 20 ounces
8. a) $3(2 - 5t)$ b) $-x - 2$ c) $x = -1$
9. a) 6 cm   b) 30.9 cm^2 (to 3 s.f.)
10. 1 hour 26 minutes (to the nearest minute)

11.

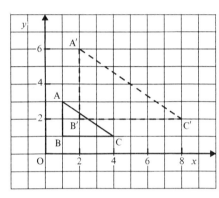

A′(2, 6)

12. a) 07.59   b) 08.31   c) 08.59   d) 08.47
     e) 11.12 arriving at 12.05
13. a) 30°   b) 10.4 cm (to 3 s.f.)
14. £88
15. £140

EXERCISE 20d   **1.** a) $\frac{1}{2}$ b) 0.0084   c) 2.7×10^5 d) 27 inches
     2. 240 km
     3. £16 and £20
     4. a) $y = 4$ b) $y = x$ c) $x = -2$ d) $y = -x$
     5. a) 8.5   b) $1\frac{1}{3}$ or 1.33 (to 3 s.f.)
         c) 7   d) $t = \dfrac{v - u}{3}$
     6. a) 400 miles   b) 120 miles   c) 210 miles   d) 100 miles
     7. a) 3 p   b) 6 st   c) $19 - 10x$
     8. £62

9. a) triangular prism

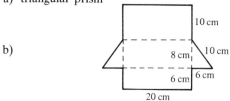

b)

c) 480 cm³

10. 6
11. a) reflection in the line BD   b) rotation of 180° about E
12. a) 450 cm²   b) 30.8 cm (to 3 s.f.)   c) 54.2°
13. $p = 40°$, $q = 100°$, $r = 80°$, $s = 10°$

14. a)

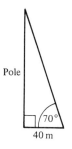

Pole

b)

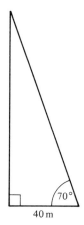

c) 110 m

15.

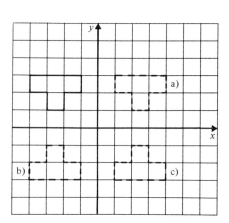

EXERCISE 20e Question 3 gives a good starting point for a general discussion of 'best buys'—for example is it always a best buy to get the pack with the cheapest unit cost?

1. £240 (£240.38 to nearest penny, but this degree of accuracy is not necessary in the context of the question)
2. 19 153
3. The packs cost 90 p a litre and the bottles cost 87 p (nearest penny) a litre; the bottles are therefore cheaper.
4. a) 10.9 cm (3 s.f.)   b) 18.5 cm (3 s.f.)
5. a) AE   b) 3
6. 8 km
7. a) 2(2x − 1)   b) 6

8. a) 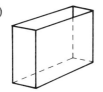   b)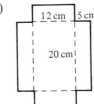

    This net gives a base 20 cm by 5 cm.

9. 565 cm³ or 565 ml (3 s.f.)
10. a) 14   b) $8\frac{1}{2}$
11. a) y(5 − y)   b) V = 18
12. a) 240 cm³   b) 4 cm²   c) $A = \dfrac{V}{l}$
13. a) (2.8, 2), (−2.8, 2)   b) (2.8, 2), (−2.8, 2)
14. a) 070°   b) 17.6 km   c) north west (315°)
15. 37.5%
16. a) false   b) true   c) cannot say
    d) false   e) true   f) false
    g) true